ELECTROM
WAVES

Roland Dobbs, DSc, is Hildred Carlile Professor of Physics at Bedford College, University of London. His research interests are in low-temperature physics and he has held positions at Brown University, Rhode Island, at the Cavendish Laboratory, Cambridge, and was first Professor of Physics and Head of Department at the University of Lancaster, where he established the low-temperature physics group. He was recently Visiting Professor at Cornell University (1984–5). He is the author of *Electricity and Magnetism* (Routledge & Kegan Paul, 1984), also published in the *Student Physics Series*.

STUDENT PHYSICS SERIES

Series Editor:
Professor R.J. Blin-Stoyle, FRS
Professor of Theoretical Physics, University of Sussex

Advisory Editors:
Professor E.R. Dobbs, *University of London*
Dr J. Goddard, *City of London Polytechnic*

The aim of the *Student Physics Series* is to cover the material required for a first degree course in physics in a series of concise, clear and readable texts. Each volume will cover one of the usual sections of the physics degree course and will concentrate on covering the essential features of the subject. The texts will thus provide a core course in physics that all students should be expected to acquire, and to which more advanced work can be related according to ability. By concentrating on the essentials, the texts should also allow a valuable perspective and accessibility not normally attainable through the more usual textbooks.

'At a time when many undergraduate textbooks illustrate inflation in poundage, both in weight and cost, an interesting countertrend is established by the introduction from Routledge of a series of small carefully written paperbacks devoted to key areas of physics. The enterprising authors are E.R. Dobbs (*Electricity and Magnetism*), B.P. Cowan (*Classical Mechanics*), R.E. Turner (*Relativity Physics*) and Paul Davies (*Quantum Mechanics*). The student is offered an account of a key area of physics summarised within an attractive small paperback, and the lecturer is given the opportunity to develop a lecture treatment around this core.' — Daphne Jackson and David Hurd, *New Scientist*

Already published

Quantum Mechanics, *P.C.W. Davies*
Electricity and Magnetism, *E.R. Dobbs*
Classical Mechanics, *B.P. Cowan*
Relativity Physics, *R.E. Turner*
Liquids and Solids, *M.T. Sprackling*

ELECTROMAGNETIC WAVES

Roland Dobbs

Hildred Carlile Professor of Physics
University of London

ROUTLEDGE & KEGAN PAUL
London, Boston, Melbourne and Henley

First published in 1985
by Routledge & Kegan Paul plc
14 Leicester Square, London WC2H 7PH, England
9 Park Street, Boston, Mass. 02108, USA
464 St Kilda Road, Melbourne,
Victoria 3004, Australia and
Broadway House, Newtown Road,
Henley-on-Thames, Oxon RG9 1EN, England

Set in Press Roman by Hope Services, Abingdon
and printed in Great Britain
by Cox & Wyman Ltd., Reading, Berks

Library of Congress Cataloging in Publication Data

Dobbs, Roland, 1924–

Electromagnetic waves.
(Student physics series)
Includes index.
1. Electromagnetic waves.   I. Title.   II. Series.
QC661.D57   1985   530.1'41   84-26712

ISBN 0-7102-0506-6

Contents

Preface

Electromagnetism began in the nineteenth century when Faraday showed electricity and magnetism were not distinct, separate phenomena, but interacted when there were time-varying electric or magnetic fields. In *Electricity and Magnetism* I have shown from first principles how Faraday's experiments led finally to Maxwell's four equations, which with the electromagnetic-force law summarise the whole of classical electromagnetism. This book therefore begins with Maxwell's equations and then uses them to study the propagation and generation of electromagnetic waves.

Physics is a subject in which the more advanced the treatment of a topic, the deeper the understanding of common occurrences that is revealed. In studying the solutions of Maxwell's equations you will find answers to such questions as: What is an electromagnetic wave? Why does a radio wave travel through space at the speed of light? How is a radio wave generated? Why does light pass through a straight tunnel when a radio wave does not? How does light travel down a curved glass fibre?

It is a remarkable fact that the classical laws of electromagnetism are fully consistent with Einstein's special theory of relativity and this is discussed in Chapter 2. The following four chapters provide solutions of Maxwell's equations for the propagation of electromagnetic waves in free space, in dielectrics, across interfaces and in conductors respectively. In Chapter 7 the generation of radio waves from dipoles and of microwaves from other antennas is explained, while the final chapter shows how these waves can be transmitted down waveguides and coaxial lines. In conclusion, the use of resonant and re-entrant cavities leads to a discussion of the classical theory of cavity radiation and its usefulness as a limiting case of the quantum theory of radiation.

The spectrum of electromagnetic radiation covers an enormous range of frequencies, from the very low frequencies (VLF) used to communicate with submerged submarines to the enormous frequencies (10^{24} Hz) associated with some cosmic rays from outer space. The complete spectrum is illustrated (opposite p. 1), where it is characterised by both the classical, wave properties of frequency (ν) and wavelength (λ) and the quantised, photon properties of energy ($h\nu$) and temperature ($h\nu/k_B$). Classical electromagnetism provides a theory of the wave properties of radiation over a wide frequency range, including for example the diffraction of X-rays by crystals, but for interactions of radiation with matter classical theory only applies in the long wavelength, low frequency, low energy ($h\nu \ll k_B$) limit. The generation of electromagnetic radiation is similarly the classical process of acceleration of electrons in producing a radio wave, where the wavelength is macroscopic, but quantum processes are involved in the production of X-rays by electronic transitions in atoms, or gamma rays by nucleonic transitions in nuclei, where the wavelengths are microscopic. The production of light by laser action is an interesting example of the combination of the classical process of reflection with the quantum process of stimulated emission. In this text the limits of classical electromagnetism are explained and the usefulness of the wave and particle properties of radiation are discussed, so that the reader is provided with an understanding of the applicability and limitations of classical theory.

SI units are used throughout and are listed for each electromagnetic quantity in Appendix 1. Since Gaussian units are still in use in some research papers on electromagnetism, Appendix 2 lists Maxwell's equations in these units and states the conversion from the Gaussian to the SI systems. The physical constants used in the text are listed in Appendix 3 with their approximate values and units. Vector calculus was introduced in *Electricity and Magnetism* and is used here from the beginning. In Appendices 4 and 5 there are summaries of the most useful relations in vector calculus and special relativity. Finally each chapter, except the first, has a set of associated exercises in Appendix 6, with answers in Appendix 7.

Acknowledgments

It is a pleasure to thank colleagues in the Universities of London and Sussex for their helpful comments and criticisms and my wife for her constant support. I am indebted especially to Mrs Sheila Pearson for her rapid production of an accurate typescript at a particularly busy time, as we were planning our move from Regent's Park to Egham Hill in the restructuring of the University of London.

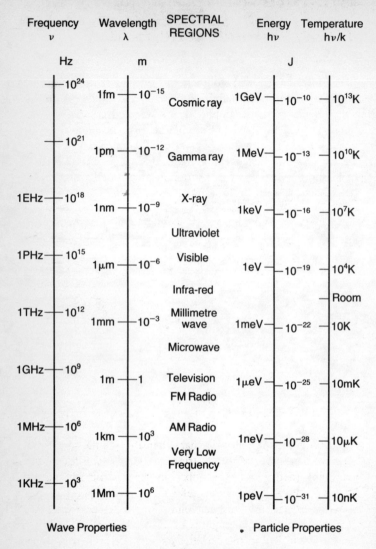

The Electromagnetic Spectrum

$[1Hz \equiv 3.00 \times 10^{8}m \equiv 4.14 \times 10^{-15}eV \equiv 4.80 \times 10^{-11} K].$

Chapter 1
The electromagnetic field

Electromagnetic theory is a triumph of classical physics. It was completed in a set of differential equations by Maxwell between 1855 and 1865. These are Maxwell's equations for the electromagnetic field. In this chapter they are first given in the form derived from first principles in *Electricity and Magnetism* in this series and then reformulated for free space and for matter.

Maxwell's equations for the electric field **E** and magnetic field **B** of any electromagnetic field at any frequency are:

$$\text{div } \mathbf{E} = \rho/\epsilon_0 \qquad\qquad [1.1]$$

$$\text{div } \mathbf{B} = 0 \qquad\qquad [1.2]$$

$$\text{curl } \mathbf{E} = -\frac{\partial \mathbf{B}}{\partial t} \qquad\qquad [1.3]$$

$$\text{curl } \mathbf{B} = \mu_0 \left(\mathbf{j} + \epsilon_0 \frac{\partial \mathbf{E}}{\partial t} \right) \qquad\qquad [1.4]$$

where ρ is the total electric charge density, $\mathbf{j}$ is the total electric current density, ϵ_0 is the electric constant and μ_0 is the magnetic constant (defined in Appendix 3). The electric and magnetic fields in Maxwell's equations refer to a classical 'point', which is conceived as an infinitesimal volume of a macroscopic field, but containing a very large number of atoms. In matter therefore the fields **E** and **B**, and the densities ρ and $\mathbf{j}$, are averages over large numbers of microscopic particles (electrons, protons, neutrons). The equations are not limited to linear, isotropic media, but apply to non-linear, anisotropic and non-homogeneous media.

In completely empty, or free, space there can be no electric charges and no electric currents, so that Maxwell's equations become:

$$\text{div } \mathbf{E} = 0 \qquad\qquad\qquad [1.5]$$

$$\text{div } \mathbf{B} = 0 \qquad\qquad\qquad [1.6]$$

$$\text{curl } \mathbf{E} = -\frac{\partial \mathbf{B}}{\partial t} \qquad\qquad\qquad [1.7]$$

$$\text{curl } \mathbf{B} = \mu_0\, \epsilon_0\, \frac{\partial \mathbf{E}}{\partial t}. \qquad\qquad\qquad [1.8]$$

The surprising result of these equations, as Maxwell first showed in 1864, is that electric and magnetic fields do not merely exist in free space, but can propagate at the speed of light over galactic distances. So using satellites modern astronomy is able to explore the universe over the entire electromagnetic spectrum from cosmic rays to long-wavelength radio waves. We shall solve equations [1.5] to [1.8] for the electric and magnetic fields of electromagnetic waves in Chapter 3.

In the presence of matter, many physicists prefer to reformulate Maxwell's equations [1.1] to [1.4] in terms of the four fields $\mathbf{E}$, $\mathbf{D}$, $\mathbf{B}$ and $\mathbf{H}$, where the electric displacement $\mathbf{D}$ and the magnetising field $\mathbf{H}$ are defined by:

$$\mathbf{D} = \epsilon_0\, \mathbf{E} + \mathbf{P} \qquad\qquad\qquad [1.9]$$

and

$$\mathbf{H} = \frac{\mathbf{B}}{\mu_0} - \mathbf{M}. \qquad\qquad\qquad [1.10]$$

Here $\mathbf{P}$ is the electric polarisation in a dielectric medium and $\mathbf{M}$ is the magnetisation in magnetic matter. The result is that equations [1.1] and [1.4] are changed, but equations [1.2] and [1.3], which do not contain any sources, remain as before. We will now show explicitly how first equation [1.1] and then equation [1.4] can be rewritten in terms of $\mathbf{D}$ and $\mathbf{H}$ for use in dielectrics and magnetic matter.

When a dielectric medium is present the charge density ρ in

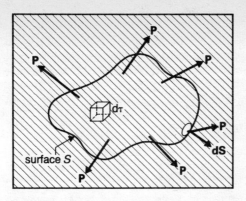

Fig. 1.1 Non-uniform polarisation of a dielectric

equation [1.1] is the sum of the density ρ_p of any polarisation charges and the density ρ_f of any free charges. Therefore equation [1.1] becomes:

$$\text{div } \epsilon_0 \mathbf{E} = \rho_p + \rho_f. \tag{1.11}$$

For an arbitrary surface S inside a dielectric (Fig. 1.1) it is the normal components of the polarisation vectors $\mathbf{P}$ that produce a surface charge. A non-uniform polarisation at the surface S therefore produces a total displacement of charge q_p across S given by:

$$q_p = \int_S \mathbf{P.dS}.$$

Since a dielectric is electrically neutral this must be compensated by a charge density $-\rho_p$ such that:

$$\int_V - \rho_p \mathrm{d}\tau = - q_p.$$

Hence the flux of $\mathbf{P}$ is given by a type of Gauss's law for polarised dielectrics:

$$\int_S \mathbf{P.dS} = - \int_V \rho_p \mathrm{d}\tau. \tag{1.12}$$

Applying Gauss's divergence theorem (Appendix 4) to this equation we have:

$$\int_V \text{div } \mathbf{P}\,\mathrm{d}\tau = -\int_V \rho_p\,\mathrm{d}\tau$$

and so

$$\text{div } \mathbf{P} = -\rho_p. \qquad [1.13]$$

Substituting for ρ_p in equation [1.11] gives:

$$\text{div } (\epsilon_0 \mathbf{E} + \mathbf{P}) = \rho_f$$

or

$$\text{div } \mathbf{D} = \rho_f. \qquad [1.14]$$

The fourth Maxwell equation, [1.4], includes a term $\partial \mathbf{E}/\partial t$ for electric fields that are varying with time. In the presence of such time-dependent fields the motion of the polarisation charges in a dielectric produces a polarisation current of density $\mathbf{j}_p$. Since charge is conserved, the outward flux of such a current density from a volume V must be equal to the rate of decrease of the polarisation charges within it:

$$\int_S \mathbf{j}_p.\mathbf{dS} = -\frac{\partial}{\partial t} \int_V \rho_p\,\mathrm{d}\tau. \qquad [1.15]$$

From equation [1.12] this becomes

$$\int_S \mathbf{j}_p.\mathbf{dS} = \frac{\partial}{\partial t} \int_S \mathbf{P}.\mathbf{dS}$$

and, since the time derivative can be taken either before or after the integration,

$$\mathbf{j}_p = \frac{\partial \mathbf{P}}{\partial t}. \qquad [1.16]$$

Applying equation [1.4] to a polarisable and magnetisable medium we must put

$$\mathbf{j} = \mathbf{j}_f + \mathbf{j}_p + \mathbf{j}_m \qquad [1.17]$$

where the total electric current density $\mathbf{j}$ is the sum of the conduction current density $\mathbf{j}_f$ due to the free charges ρ_f, the polarisation current density $\mathbf{j}_p$ due to the polarisation charges ρ_p, and the magnetisation current density $\mathbf{j}_m$ associated with magnetised matter. This arises from the atomic currents inside the matter which are equivalent to small magnetic dipoles.

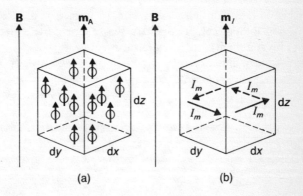

Fig. 1.2 (a) An elementary volume of uniformly magnetised matter is equivalent to (b) a surface magnetisation current I_m

Magnetisation of matter by applied magnetic fields is a similar phenomenon to the polarisation of matter by applied electric fields. In Fig. 1.2(a) an elementary cube $\mathrm{d}x\mathrm{d}y\mathrm{d}z$ of a paramagnetic has been magnetised in the uniform applied field $\mathbf{B}$ and the aligned magnetic dipoles add to a magnetic moment $\mathbf{m}_A$. This can be exactly equivalent to a single current loop, shown in Fig. 1.2(b), where a current I_m around the volume element produces a magnetic moment:

$$m_I = I_m \ \mathrm{d}x\mathrm{d}y = m_A .$$

By definition the magnetisation $\mathbf{M}$ of the elementary volume is the magnetic moment $\mathbf{m}_A$ per unit volume, so that its magnitude is:

$$M = \frac{m_A}{\mathrm{d}x\mathrm{d}y\mathrm{d}z} = \frac{I_m}{\mathrm{d}z} = i_m$$

where i_m is the surface current density or surface current per unit length normal to the current. The uniform magnetisation M of a block can thus be replaced by an equivalent surface current density i_m which acts in the direction given by:

$$\mathbf{M} \times \hat{\mathbf{n}} = \mathbf{i}_m \qquad [1.18]$$

where $\hat{\mathbf{n}}$ is the outward normal of the surface of the block containing the current. In this case the volume current density $\mathbf{j}_m$ is zero and there is only a surface current density $\mathbf{i}_m$.

For a non-uniformly magnetised material, however, there is also an equivalent current density $\mathbf{j}_m$, by analogy with Ampère's law:

$$\oint_C \frac{\mathbf{B}}{\mu_0} \cdot \mathbf{ds} = \int_S \mathbf{j} \cdot \mathbf{dS} \qquad [1.19]$$

namely

$$\oint_C \mathbf{M} \cdot \mathbf{ds} = \int_S \mathbf{j}_m \cdot \mathbf{dS}. \qquad [1.20]$$

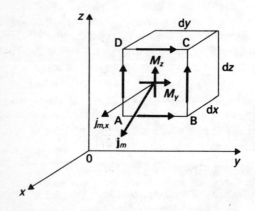

Fig. 1.3 An elementary volume of non-uniform magnetisation is equivalent to a volume current density $\mathbf{j}_m$

This is illustrated in Fig. 1.3, where for the contour ABCD:

$$\oint_C \mathbf{M.ds} = \left(M_y - \frac{\partial M_y}{\partial z}\frac{\mathrm{d}z}{2}\right)\ \mathrm{d}y + \left(M_z + \frac{\partial M_z}{\partial y}\frac{\mathrm{d}y}{2}\right)\ \mathrm{d}z$$

$$- \left(M_y + \frac{\partial M_y}{\partial z}\frac{\mathrm{d}z}{2}\right)\ \mathrm{d}y - \left(M_z - \frac{\partial M_z}{\partial y}\frac{\mathrm{d}y}{2}\right)\ \mathrm{d}z$$

$$= -\frac{\partial M_y}{\partial z}\ \mathrm{d}y\mathrm{d}z + \frac{\partial M_z}{\partial y}\ \mathrm{d}y\mathrm{d}z$$

$$= (\mathrm{curl}\ \mathbf{M})_x\ \mathrm{d}y\mathrm{d}z.$$

However for this contour the flux of $\mathbf{j}_m = j_{m,x}\ \mathrm{d}y\mathrm{d}z$, so that:

$$j_{m,x} = (\mathrm{curl}\ \mathbf{M})_x.$$

Similarly for the other faces of the cube $j_{m,y} = (\mathrm{curl}\ \mathbf{M})_y$ and $j_{m,z} = (\mathrm{curl}\ \mathbf{M})_z$, and the equivalent current density is:

$$\mathbf{j}_m = \mathrm{curl}\ \mathbf{M} \qquad [1.21]$$

Combining equations [1.16], [1.17] and [1.21], we have for the total current density $\mathbf{j}$ of equation [1.4]:

$$\mathbf{j} = \mathbf{j}_f + \frac{\partial \mathbf{P}}{\partial t} + \mathrm{curl}\ \mathbf{M} \qquad [1.22]$$

and so Maxwell's fourth equation becomes:

$$\mathrm{curl}\left(\frac{\mathbf{B}}{\mu_0}\right) = \mathbf{j}_f + \frac{\partial \mathbf{P}}{\partial t} + \mathrm{curl}\ \mathbf{M} + \epsilon_0\frac{\partial \mathbf{E}}{\partial t}$$

or

$$\mathrm{curl}\left(\frac{\mathbf{B}}{\mu_0} - M\right) = \mathbf{j}_f + \left(\epsilon_0\frac{\partial \mathbf{E}}{\partial t} + \frac{\partial \mathbf{P}}{\partial t}\right).$$

From the definitions of $\mathbf{D}$ and $\mathbf{H}$ in equations [1.9] and [1.10] it therefore follows that:

$$\mathrm{curl}\ \mathbf{H} = \mathbf{j}_f + \frac{\partial \mathbf{D}}{\partial t}. \qquad [1.23]$$

We conclude that for a polarisable, magnetisable medium the four Maxwell equations can also be written:

$$\text{div }\mathbf{D} = \rho_f \qquad\qquad\qquad [1.14]$$

$$\text{div }\mathbf{B} = 0 \qquad\qquad\qquad [1.2]$$

$$\text{curl }\mathbf{E} = -\frac{\partial \mathbf{B}}{\partial t} \qquad\qquad\qquad [1.3]$$

$$\text{curl }\mathbf{H} = \mathbf{j}_f + \frac{\partial \mathbf{D}}{\partial t} \qquad\qquad\qquad [1.23]$$

and we shall use either this set or equations [1.1] to [1.4] as appropriate in this book. Both sets of equations apply to non-linear, anisotropic, non-homogeneous media, providing the definitions for $\mathbf{D}$ and $\mathbf{H}$ are those given in equations [1.9] and [1.10]. The alternative definitions in terms of the dimensionless dielectric constant (relative permittivity) ϵ_r and relative permeability μ_r:

$$\mathbf{B} = \mu_r \mu_0 \mathbf{H} \qquad\qquad\qquad [1.24]$$

$$\mathbf{D} = \epsilon_r \epsilon_0 \mathbf{E} \qquad\qquad\qquad [1.25]$$

are particularly useful in linear, isotropic materials. Then the magnetisation $\mathbf{M}$ is proportional to $\mathbf{H}$ and the polarisation $\mathbf{P}$ is proportional to $\mathbf{E}$ and so μ_r, ϵ_r are scalars. In anisotropic materials, such as piezoelectric crystals, the dielectric constant becomes a tensor:

$$\epsilon_{\alpha\beta} = \frac{1}{\epsilon_0} \frac{\partial D_\alpha}{\partial E_\beta} \qquad\qquad\qquad [1.26]$$

while in non-linear materials, such as ferromagnetics, the permeability varies over the hysteresis loop and becomes a differential:

$$\mu_r(B, H) = \frac{1}{\mu_0} \frac{dB}{dH}. \qquad\qquad\qquad [1.27]$$

Chapter 2
Electromagnetism and relativity

In this chapter we show first that the magnetic field **B** arises naturally from a Lorentz transformation of the electric force in Coulomb's law and so we can investigate the electric and magnetic fields of rapidly moving charges. Then by introducing a vector potential **A** subject to the Lorentz gauge condition we find a remarkable similarity between the equations of electrostatics, expressed in terms of the scalars ϕ (potential) and ρ, and the equations of magnetostatics in terms of the vectors **A** and **j**. Finally we show, using a four-dimensional notation, that it is possible to reduce Maxwell's four equations to just one equation which expresses directly the invariance of electromagnetism under the Lorentz transformation.

2.1 Lorentz transformations

In Einstein's special theory of relativity (see *Relativity Physics* by R. Turner, in this series) Newton's laws of motion are modified so that instead of a Galilean transformation, valid for mechanical phenomena when relative speeds are much less than the speed of light, c, a Lorentz transformation valid for all types of physical phenomena at all speeds is required. As a consequence of this all physical laws must be *invariant* under a Lorentz transformation.

A simple example to show the difference between Galilean and Lorentz transformations is to consider the coordinates of a point P' in an inertial frame S' (x', y', z') moving with speed u (parallel to $0x$) relative to an inertial frame S (x, y, z), as shown in Fig. 2.1(a). The transformations are then:

Galilean transformations	Lorentz transformations

$$x' = x - ut \qquad\qquad x' = \gamma (x - ut)$$
$$y' = y \qquad\qquad\qquad y' = y \qquad\qquad\qquad [2.1]$$
$$z' = z' \qquad\qquad\qquad z' = z$$
$$t' = t \qquad\qquad\qquad t' = \gamma \{t - (u/c^2)x\}$$

where $\gamma = 1/\{1 - (u^2/c^2)\}^{\frac{1}{2}} = 1/(1 - \beta^2)^{\frac{1}{2}} \geqslant 1$. As a result of applying relativity theory to an object moving with a speed u relative to an observer the following transformations are found:

1. the FitzGerald contraction of length L_0 to $L = L_0/\gamma$;
2. the dilatation of a time interval T_0 to $T = \gamma T_0$;
3. the increase of a rest mass m_0 to $m = \gamma m_0$.

From these it follows that relativistic energy $U = \gamma m_0 c^2$, relativistic momentum $\mathbf{p} = (\gamma m_0)\,\mathbf{v}$ and that a force $\mathbf{F}$ in a frame S transforms to a force $\mathbf{F}' = \gamma \mathbf{F}$ in a moving frame S'.

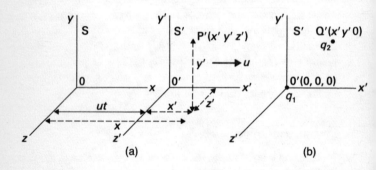

Fig. 2.1 Frame S' (x', y', z') is moving at speed u along Ox and has moved a distance ut from the S frame (x, y, z) during the time t. The coordinates of P' are (x', y', z') and of Q' $(x', y', 0)$

The basic quantities in electromagnetism are electric charge q, electric charge density ρ and electric current density $\mathbf{j}$. What happens to these quantities when we observe them in a moving frame? We might expect q to transform to γq like mass, or to q/γ like a length. In fact this does not occur. Electric charge, unlike mass, is *invariant* at all speeds. The best evidence for this comes from measurements of the ratio of the electronic charge-to-mass ratio, e/m, for high-energy electrons from accelerators that operate at GeV energies, where the electron's speed can be within 1 part in 10^8 of c. When the increase of mass from m_0 to γm_0 is allowed for, there is no change in the value of e.

In order to find how charge density ρ and current density $\mathbf{j} = \rho\mathbf{v}$ transform, we require the transformations for an element of volume $d\tau_0$ and a velocity. For simplicity let us assume we place $d\tau_0$ at P' in the S' frame (Fig. 2.1(a)) and allow it to move at a speed $v_x{}'$ in this frame parallel to the x' axis. It can readily be shown from the Lorentz transformations of length and time in equations [2.1] that $v_x{}'$ is related to v_x in the S frame by:

$$v_x{}' = \frac{v_x - u}{1 - (v_x u/c^2)}.$$ [2.2]

In the S' frame the volume element will contract only in the x direction so that it becomes:

$$d\tau' = d\tau_0 \left\{ 1 - \left(\frac{v_x{}'}{c}\right)^2 \right\}^{1/2}$$

while in the S frame it will appear to be:

$$d\tau = d\tau_0 \left\{ 1 - \left(\frac{v_x}{c}\right)^2 \right\}^{1/2}.$$

Therefore

$$\frac{d\tau'}{d\tau} = \left\{ \frac{1 - \left(\dfrac{v_x{}'}{c}\right)^2}{1 - \left(\dfrac{v_x}{c}\right)^2} \right\}^{1/2}$$

and when $v_x{}'$ is substituted from equation [2.2] the ratio simplifies to:

$$\frac{d\tau'}{d\tau} = \frac{1}{\gamma \left\{ 1 - (v_x u/c^2) \right\}}.$$ [2.3]

Using equations [2.2] and [2.3] we can now transform a charge density ρ' in the S' frame to a charge density ρ in the S frame. The charge q will be invariant, so that:

$$q = \rho d\tau = \rho' d\tau'$$

and therefore

$$\frac{\rho'}{\rho} = \frac{d\tau}{d\tau'} = \gamma \left(1 - \frac{v_x u}{c^2}\right).$$

This can more usefully be expressed in terms of the x-component of the current density $\mathbf{j}$, since $j_x = \rho v_x$ and so:

$$\rho' = \gamma \left(\rho - \frac{u j_x}{c^2}\right). \tag{2.4}$$

On the other hand:

$$j_x' = \rho' v_x' = \gamma \left(\rho - \frac{u j_x}{c^2}\right) \left\{\frac{v_x - u}{1 - (v_x u/c^2)}\right\}$$

and this simplifies to:

$$j_x' = \gamma (j_x - u\rho). \tag{2.5}$$

Since the only component of $\mathbf{v}$ is v_x:

$$j_y' = j_y \text{ and } j_z' = j_z. \tag{2.6}$$

When we compare equations [2.4], [2.5] and [2.6] with the Lorentz transformations for x', y', z' and t' in equations [2.1], we see that the current density $\mathbf{j}$ and charge density ρ transform just like the position vector $\mathbf{r}$ and the time t. Another way of putting it is that the four-vector $j_\nu \equiv (\mathbf{j}, ic\rho)$ and its invariant $j_\nu^2 = j^2 - c^2\rho^2$ in electromagnetism correspond to the four-vector $r_\nu = (\mathbf{r}, ict)$ and its invariant $r_\nu^2 = r^2 - c^2 t^2$ in mechanics, where we denote the Einstein summation convention over four coordinates by the Greek letter ν (for example, $j_\nu^2 \equiv j_1^2 + j_2^2 + j_3^2 + j_4^2$, where $j_1 = j_x, j_2 = j_y, j_3 = j_z, j_4 = ic\rho$).

2.2 Fields of moving charges

Origin of B

We are now in a position to see what happens when we transform the Coulomb force between two charges at rest in a moving frame S' back into the laboratory frame S. Let us put one charge q_1 at

$0'$ in Fig. 2.1(b) and the other q_2 at Q' so that their coordinates in the S' frame are q_1 $(0, 0, 0)$ and q_2 $(x', y', 0)$. In this frame the Coulomb force $\mathbf{F}'$ has components:

$$F_x' = \frac{q_1 q_2 x'}{4\pi\epsilon_0 r'^3}, \quad F_y' = \frac{q_1 q_2 y'}{4\pi\epsilon_0 r'^3}, \quad F_z' = 0. \quad [2.7]$$

To simplify the calculation of the force $\mathbf{F}$ in the S frame we will compute it at time $t = 0$, when q_1 is at 0 and the two frames coincide.

Since the relative motion of S' with respect to S is along $0x$, only the y and z components of $\mathbf{F}'$ are contracted and:

$$F_x = F_x', \quad F_y = F_y'/\gamma, \quad F_z = F_z'/\gamma. \quad [2.8]$$

The force $\mathbf{F}$ therefore has components:

$$F_x = \frac{q_1 q_2 x'}{4\pi\epsilon_0 (x'^2 + y'^2)^{3/2}} \text{ and } F_y = \frac{q_1 q_2 y'}{4\pi\epsilon_0 \gamma (x'^2 + y'^2)^{3/2}}.$$

Substituting for x', y' at $t = 0$ from equations [2.1] and multiplying by γ, these become:

$$F_x = \frac{\gamma q_1 q_2 x}{4\pi\epsilon_0 (\gamma^2 x^2 + y^2)^{3/2}}, \quad F_y = \frac{\gamma q_1 q_2 y}{4\pi\epsilon_0 (\gamma^2 x^2 + y^2)^{3/2}} \left(1 - \frac{u^2}{c^2}\right).$$

At $t = 0$, q_2 is at $\mathbf{r} = x\hat{\mathbf{i}} + y\hat{\mathbf{j}}$, so we can put (writing $x\hat{\mathbf{i}} = \mathbf{r} - y\hat{\mathbf{j}}$):

$$\mathbf{F} = \frac{\gamma q_1 q_2 \mathbf{r}}{4\pi\epsilon_0 (\gamma^2 x^2 + y^2)^{3/2}} - \frac{\gamma q_1 q_2 u^2 y\mathbf{j}}{4\pi\epsilon_0 c^2 (\gamma^2 x^2 + y^2)^{3/2}}.$$

Alternatively, since $\mathbf{u} = u\hat{\mathbf{i}}$ and $\hat{\mathbf{i}} \times \hat{\mathbf{k}} = -\hat{\mathbf{j}}$, we can write:

$$\mathbf{F} = q_2 \left\{ \frac{\gamma q_1 \mathbf{r}}{4\pi\epsilon_0 (\gamma^2 x^2 + y^2)^{3/2}} + \frac{\mathbf{u} \times \gamma q_1 uy\hat{\mathbf{k}}}{4\pi\epsilon_0 c^2 (\gamma^2 x^2 + y^2)^{3/2}} \right\}.$$

$$[2.9]$$

This equation is just the Lorentz force law:

$$\mathbf{F} = q_2 (\mathbf{E} + \mathbf{u} \times \mathbf{B}) \quad [2.10]$$

where

$$\mathbf{E} = \frac{\gamma q_1 \mathbf{r}}{4\pi\epsilon_0 (\gamma^2 x^2 + y^2)^{3/2}} \text{ and } \mathbf{B} = \frac{\mu_0 \gamma q_1 uy\hat{\mathbf{k}}}{4\pi (\gamma^2 x^2 + y^2)^{3/2}}. \quad [2.11]$$

These expressions are readily seen to have the familiar form:

$$\mathbf{E_0} = \left(\frac{q}{4\pi\epsilon_0 r^2}\right) \hat{\mathbf{r}} \text{ and } \mathbf{B_0} = \left(\frac{\mu_0}{4\pi}\right) \left(\frac{\hat{\mathbf{j}} \times \hat{\mathbf{r}}}{r^2}\right)$$

when u is small and $\gamma \cong 1$. The relationships between $\mathbf{F}$, $\mathbf{E}$ and $\mathbf{B}$ are shown in Fig. 2.2.

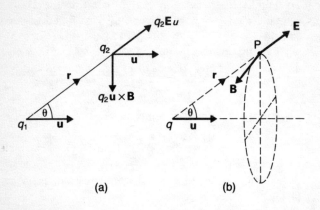

Fig. 2.2 (a) The force $\mathbf{F}$ between charges q_1 and q_2 moving at the same velocity $\mathbf{u}$ is the vector sum of an electric force $q_2 \mathbf{E}_u$ and a magnetic force $q_2 \mathbf{u} \times \mathbf{B}$. (b) The electric field $\mathbf{E}$ and magnetic field $\mathbf{B}$ at P (r, θ) due to a charge q moving at velocity $\mathbf{u}$

This straightforward application of the special theory of relativity has therefore shown that an electric force $\mathbf{F}'$ in the moving frame is transformed into the Lorentz force $\mathbf{F}$ in the laboratory frame. The magnetic field $\mathbf{B}$, which is associated with moving charges and electric currents in elementary theory, is not a separate phenomenon but a relativistic transformation of a moving electric field. We will now consider how these fields change when charges are travelling at relativistic speeds.

Electric fields

The electric field $\mathbf{E}_u$ of a charge moving at speed u is radial (Fig. 2.2(a)), just as for a stationary charge, but its magnitude is a function of θ that depends on the ratio $\beta = u/c$. This is readily seen for the limiting cases of $\theta = 0$ and $\pi/2$. From equation [2.11] and Fig. 2.2(a), when $\theta = 0$, $x = r$, $y = 0$ and so the magnetic field is zero and the electric field is:

$$\mathbf{E}_u = \frac{1}{\gamma^2}\,\mathbf{E}_0.$$

Clearly as the speed u increases towards c, so the electric field also tends to zero. On the other hand for $\theta = \pi/2$, $x = 0$, $y = r$ and the electric field is:

$$\mathbf{E}_u = \gamma\mathbf{E}_0$$

and this increases as u increases towards c. At this angle the electric and magnetic forces are in direct opposition and as u increases towards c the total force (Fig. 2.2(a)) on q_2 due to q_1 tends to zero. The changes in $E_u\,(\theta)$ at other angles as u increases are shown in Fig. 2.3(a) for several values of $\beta = u/c$.

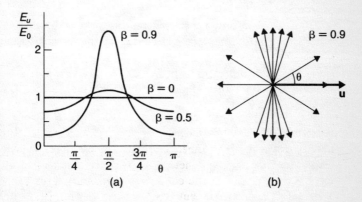

Fig. 2.3 (a) The electric field E_u/E_0 at angle θ to velocity **u** of charge, as seen by a stationary observer, for $\beta = u/c = 0$, 0.5 and 0.9. (b) Lines of the electric field $\mathbf{E}_u$ from a charge at velocity **u** and $\beta = 0.9$, as seen by a stationary observer

It is seen that the effect is significant when u is $0.5c$, the speed an electron reaches when accelerated through 80 keV. At the higher speed of $0.9c$ a stationary observer would find a distinctly non-uniform, radial electric field, as shown in Fig. 2.3(b). Ultimately this field exists only in a thin disc normal to the direction of motion of the charge.

Magnetic fields

The magnetic field **B** of a moving charge is always normal to the velocity **u** of the charge and so lines of **B** are circles centred on the trajectory of **u** (Fig. 2.4(a)). A stationary charge has no magnetic field and, as $\beta = u/c$ increases, the magnetic field at first increases at all angles (Fig. 2.4(b)) but for $\beta > 0.5$, the magnetic field becomes increasingly concentrated into a thin disc normal to the direction of motion of the charge. Thus at these high relativistic speeds both the electric and the magnetic fields are concentrated into the same plane normal to **u**.

General case

So far we have only considered the case where the charges are both moving at the same speed, that of the moving frame. In general the velocity **u** of the moving frame (O′ relative to O in Fig. 2.5) will differ from the velocity **v** of a charge at P in the stationary (laboratory) frame. In this case the distance O′P in the laboratory frame after time t is:

$$\mathbf{r} = (x - ut)\,\hat{\mathbf{i}} + y\hat{\mathbf{j}} + z\hat{\mathbf{k}} \qquad [2.12]$$

and, using the Lorentz transformations of equations [2.1] this distance in the moving frame is:

$$\mathbf{r}' = \gamma\,(x - ut)\,\hat{\mathbf{i}} + y\hat{\mathbf{j}} + z\hat{\mathbf{k}}. \qquad [2.13]$$

In order to find the force law for this moving charge we consider, as before, the force exerted by a charge, q_1 at O′ $(0,0,0)$ on a charge q_2 at P (x', y', z'), where the coordinates are in the moving frame where q_1 is stationary. In this frame the Coulomb force **F**′ is then:

$$\mathbf{F}' = \frac{q_1 q_2}{4\pi\epsilon_0 r'^3}\,\{x'\hat{\mathbf{i}} + y'\hat{\mathbf{j}} + z'\hat{\mathbf{k}}\}. \qquad [2.14]$$

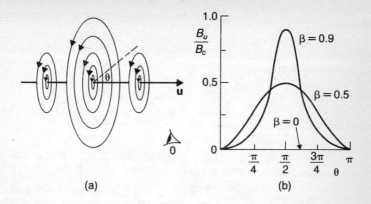

Fig. 2.4 (a) Lines of the magnetic field $\mathbf{B}_u$ from a charge at velocity $\mathbf{u}$ and speed $\beta = 0.5$, as seen by a stationary observer O. (b) The magnetic field B_u/B_c at angle θ to velocity $\mathbf{u}$ of the charge, as seen by a stationary observer, for $\beta = 0, 0.5$ and 0.9, and $B_c = \mu_0 qc/4\pi r^2$

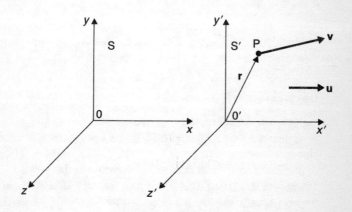

Fig. 2.5 The frame S' is moving at speed u along $0x$ relative to the laboratory frame S and its origin has moved from 0 to $0'$ in time t. The point $P(x, y, z)$ is moving at a velocity $\mathbf{v}$ in the laboratory frame, where $\mathbf{v}$ differs in magnitude and direction from $\mathbf{u}$

It is left as an exercise for the reader (Exercise 2.1, Appendix 6) using the Lorentz transformations for the coordinates, the velocities and the components of the force (Appendix 5) to show that the Coulomb force $\mathbf{F}'$ transforms into the Lorentz force $\mathbf{F}$ in the laboratory frame:

$$\mathbf{F} = q_2 \ \{\mathbf{E} + (\mathbf{v} \times \mathbf{B})\} \tag{2.15}$$

where

$$\mathbf{E} = \frac{\gamma q_1 \mathbf{r}}{4\pi\epsilon_0 r'^3} \text{ and } \mathbf{B} = \left(\frac{\mu_0}{4\pi}\right) \frac{\gamma q_1 u \left(-z\hat{\mathbf{j}} + y\hat{\mathbf{k}}\right)}{r'^3} . \tag{2.16}$$

By comparing equations [2.15] and [2.10] we see that the magnetic force in the laboratory frame due to q_1 on q_2 at P is proportional to the velocity $\mathbf{v}$ *in that frame*, as well as depending on the speed of q_1 through the factor γu. We conclude that the magnetic force is:

1. zero in a given frame of reference, unless $\mathbf{v}$ is finite in that frame;
2. independent of the component of $\mathbf{v}$ normal to $\mathbf{u}$;
3. normal to $\mathbf{v}$ and so does no work.

The last point is used extensively in particle physics when a magnet deflects a beam of charged particles without changing their kinetic energy.

Current in a wire

We can use the concepts of special relativity to see how a current I in a long, thin metal wire (Fig. 2.6) produces a force on a charge q moving with a velocity $\mathbf{v}$ relative to the wire. The wire is stationary in the laboratory (S) frame and in this frame there is charge neutrality, so that the linear charge density λ_p of the positive ions is exactly equal and opposite to the linear charge density λ_n of the conduction electrons, i.e.

$$\lambda_p + \lambda_n = 0. \tag{2.17}$$

The conduction electrons have a small drift velocity $\mathbf{u}$ along the wire and are stationary in the moving (S') frame, which coincides

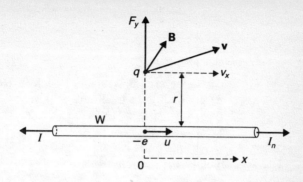

Fig. 2.6 A wire W carrying a conventional current I is at a distance r from a positive charge q moving with velocity **v**. The conduction electrons drifting at speed u parallel to the x axis produce an electron current I_n which exerts a force $F_y = qv_xB$ on q

In the laboratory frame the positive ions exert a force F_y on q given by:

$$F_y = qE_p = q\lambda_p/(2\pi\epsilon_0 r) \qquad [2.18]$$

where r is the radial distance of q from the wire. Similarly, in the moving frame the conduction electrons with linear density λ'_n exert a force F'_y given by:

$$F'_y = q\lambda'_n/(2\pi\epsilon_0 r) \qquad [2.19]$$

since q, r are invariant. An observer in this frame would measure a total electronic charge of $\lambda'_n L$, where the length L has contracted from L_0 to L_0/γ by the FitzGerald contraction. Therefore:

$$\lambda'_n = \gamma\lambda_n \qquad [2.20]$$

and

$$F'_y = q\gamma\lambda_n/(2\pi\epsilon_0 r). \qquad [2.21]$$

Using the Lorentz transformation for a force (Appendix 5) this becomes:

$$F_y = \frac{q\lambda_n}{2\pi\epsilon_0 r} \left\{ 1 - \frac{uv_x}{c^2} \right\}$$

or

$$F_y = \frac{q}{2\pi\epsilon_0 r} \left\{ \lambda_n - \left(\frac{v_x}{c^2} \right) I_n \right\}$$ [2.22]

where $I_n = \lambda_n u$ is the electron current. Therefore, combining equations [2.18] and [2.22], the total force on q is:

$$F_y = \frac{q}{2\pi\epsilon_0 r} \left\{ \lambda_p + \lambda_n - \frac{v_x I_n}{c^2} \right\}$$

and using equation [2.17] this is just:

$$F_y = -\frac{q v_x I_n}{2\pi\epsilon_0 c^2 r} = -\frac{\mu_0 q v_x I_n}{2\pi r}.$$ [2.23]

The electric fields due to the positive ions and the conduction electrons cancel perfectly and the remaining force can be recognised as the Lorentz force $q\mathbf{v} \times \mathbf{B}$, where $\mathbf{B} = (\mu_0 I/2\pi r)\,\hat{\theta}$ for a conventional current $I = -\lambda_n u = -I_n$. We now see that the magnetic field of a current in a wire results from the relativistic transformation of the electric field of the moving electrons despite the fact that typically the drift velocity of such electrons is about 10^{-4} ms^{-1}, so that $\gamma = 1$ to an accuracy of 1 part in 10^{25}! For example a current of 1 A in a copper wire of cross sectional area 1 mm^2 has a linear charge density of about:

$$\lambda_n = -10^{29} \times 10^{-6} \times 1.6 \times 10^{-19} = -1.6 \times 10^4 \text{ C m}^{-1}$$

while if q is an electron in a second wire and drift velocity $v_x = -10^{-4}$ m s^{-1}, then:

$$-\frac{v_x I_n}{c^2} = \frac{10^{-4}}{9 \times 10^{16}} = 1.1 \times 10^{-21} \text{ C m}^{-1}.$$

This confirms that in equation [2.22] the first term is about 10^{25} as large as the second term, but since λ_n is cancelled *perfectly* by λ_p, only the small **B** term remains.

Of course, the force between two current-carrying wires is appreciable only because the second wire has also, say, 10^{29}

electrons per m^3. In fact the force of attraction between two long, thin, parallel wires each carrying 1 A in the same direction and places 1 m apart is exactly 2×10^{-7} N m^{-1}, from the definition of the ampere.

2.3 Vector potentials

In electrostatics it is often the case that to find the electric field **E** from a distribution of charges $\rho \, d\tau$, it is easier to find first the electric scalar potential ϕ from an integral such as:

$$\phi(1) = \frac{1}{4\pi\epsilon_0} \int_{\substack{\text{all} \\ \text{space}}} \frac{\rho(2) \, d\tau_2}{r_{12}} \qquad [2.24]$$

and then compute the electric field from:

$$\mathbf{E} = -\operatorname{grad} \phi. \qquad [2.25]$$

In electromagnetism a similar procedure for finding the magnetic field **B** from a distribution of moving charges is possible in terms of the magnetic vector potential, **A**. Since **B** is always a divergence-free field, by equation [1.2], we can always write:

$$\mathbf{B} = \operatorname{curl} \mathbf{A} \qquad [2.26]$$

which makes

$$\operatorname{div} \mathbf{B} = \operatorname{div} \operatorname{curl} \mathbf{A} = \nabla \cdot (\nabla \times \mathbf{A}) = 0.$$

Moving charge

We have seen that a charge q travelling at speed u along the x axis and passing through the origin at $t = 0$ (Fig. 2.5) produces electric and magnetic fields at P given by equation [2.16] (we have dropped the subscript 1 here). We shall now show that the vector potential for this moving charge is:

$$\mathbf{A} = \frac{\mu_0 \gamma q u}{4\pi (r'^2)^{1/2}} \, \mathbf{i} \qquad [2.27]$$

where r' in the moving frame is the Lorentz transform of r in the laboratory frame and, by equation [2.13],

$$r'^2 = \gamma^2 (x - ut)^2 + y^2 + z^2. \qquad [2.28]$$

By definition:

$$\mathbf{B} = \text{curl}\,\mathbf{A} = \left(\frac{\partial A_z}{\partial y} - \frac{\partial A_y}{\partial z}\right)\hat{\mathbf{i}} + \left(\frac{\partial A_x}{\partial z} - \frac{\partial A_z}{\partial x}\right)\hat{\mathbf{j}} + \left(\frac{\partial A_y}{\partial x} - \frac{\partial A_x}{\partial y}\right)\hat{\mathbf{k}}$$

and so in this case:

$$\mathbf{B} = \frac{\partial A_x}{\partial z}\hat{\mathbf{j}} - \frac{\partial A_x}{\partial y}\hat{\mathbf{k}}$$

$$= \frac{\mu_0 \gamma q u}{4\pi}\left\{-\frac{1}{2}\cdot\frac{2z}{(r'^2)^{3/2}}\hat{\mathbf{j}} + \frac{1}{2}\frac{2y}{(r'^2)^{3/2}}\hat{\mathbf{k}}\right\}$$

$$= \frac{\mu_0 \gamma q u}{4\pi(r'^3)}(-z\hat{\mathbf{j}} + y\hat{\mathbf{k}})$$

exactly as found before in equation [2.16]. Therefore the vector potential $\mathbf{A}$ of a moving charge (Fig. 2.7(a)) is parallel to the velocity vector of the charge and varies as r^{-1}.

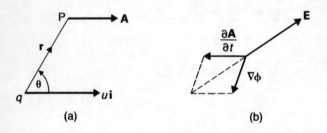

Fig 2.7 (a) Vector potential and (b) electric field of a moving charge

When a charge is moving its electric field is no longer given by equation [2.25] but by:

$$\mathbf{E} = -\,\text{grad}\,\phi - \frac{\partial A}{\partial t} \qquad [2.29]$$

which, with equation [2.26] and the identity curl grad $\phi = 0$, is

Maxwell's equation [1.3]. We can see that this is correct for the charge in Fig. 2.7(a), where **A** is given by equation [2.27] and the scalar potential is:

$$\phi = \frac{\gamma q}{4\pi\epsilon_0 r'}.$$ [2.30]

In full:

$$\mathbf{E} = -\frac{\partial\phi}{\partial x}\,\hat{\mathbf{i}} - \frac{\partial\phi}{\partial y}\,\hat{\mathbf{j}} - \frac{\partial\phi}{\partial z}\,\hat{\mathbf{k}} - \frac{\partial\mathbf{A}}{\partial t}$$

$$= \frac{\gamma q}{4\pi\epsilon_0\,(r'^3)}\left\{[\gamma^2\,(x-ut)\,\hat{\mathbf{i}} + y\hat{\mathbf{j}} + z\hat{\mathbf{k}}]\right.$$

$$\left. - \mu_0\epsilon_0 u^2\gamma^2\,(x-ut)\,\hat{\mathbf{i}}\right\}$$

since $\partial\,(r'^2)/\partial t = -2\gamma^2 u\,(x-ut)$. Hence:

$$\mathbf{E} = \frac{\gamma q}{4\pi\epsilon_0\,(r'^3)}\,\mathbf{r}$$

since $\gamma^2 - \gamma^2(u^2/c^2) = \gamma^2(1-\beta^2) = 1$, exactly as before in equation [2.16].

Four-vector equations

The potentials **A** and ϕ given in equations [2.26] and [2.29] are not unique but would still satisfy these equations if **A** was $(\mathbf{A} + \text{grad }\psi)$ and ϕ was $(\phi + \phi_0)$ for example. Lorentz showed that if we choose the gauge:

$$\text{div }\mathbf{A} = -\frac{1}{c^2}\,\frac{\partial\phi}{\partial t}$$ [2.31]

then Maxwell's equations can be expressed in a particularly simple form. Putting equations [2.29] and [2.31] into the first Maxwell equation:

$$\text{div }\mathbf{E} = \rho/\epsilon_0$$ [1.1]

we obtain

$$-\nabla^2\phi - \frac{\partial}{\partial t}(\text{div }\mathbf{A}) = \frac{\rho}{\epsilon_0}$$

and so

$$\nabla^2\phi - \frac{1}{c^2}\frac{\partial^2\phi}{\partial t^2} = -\frac{\rho}{\epsilon_0}.$$ [2.32]

Similarly putting equations [2.26], [2.29] and [2.31] into the fourth Maxwell equation:

$$\text{curl }\mathbf{B} = \mu_0\left(\mathbf{j} + \epsilon_0\frac{\partial\mathbf{E}}{\partial t}\right)$$ [1.4]

we obtain:

$$\text{grad div }\mathbf{A} - \nabla^2\mathbf{A} = \mu_0\mathbf{j} - \frac{1}{c^2}\frac{\partial}{\partial t}(\text{grad }\phi) - \frac{1}{c^2}\frac{\partial^2\mathbf{A}}{\partial t^2}$$

and so:

$$\nabla^2\mathbf{A} - \frac{1}{c^2}\frac{\partial^2\mathbf{A}}{\partial t^2} = -\mu_0\mathbf{j}.$$ [2.33]

In the four dimensions of special relativity, the Laplacian operator ∇^2 is replaced by the D'Alembertian operator:

$$\Box = \nabla^2 - \frac{1}{c^2}\frac{\partial^2}{\partial t^2}$$ [2.34]

so that equations [2.32] and [2.33] can be written:

$$\Box\phi = -\rho/\epsilon_0, \quad \Box\mathbf{A} = -\mu_0\mathbf{j}.$$ [2.35]

We have already seen (section 2.1) that

$$j_\nu \equiv (\mathbf{j}, ic\rho)$$ [2.36]

is a four-vector and so corresponds to the right-hand side of the four equations that form [2.35] divided by ϵ_0. The D'Alembertian, like the Laplacian, is the same for all coordinate systems, so the quantities A_x, A_y, A_z, ϕ must also form a four-potential:

$$A_\nu \equiv (\mathbf{A}, i\phi/c).$$ [2.37]

The simplicity of Maxwell's equations is now apparent, since we can write equations [2.33] in their invariant, relativistic form as:

$$\square A_\nu = -\mu_0 j_\nu. \qquad [2.38]$$

Similarly, using the four-dimensional vector operator $\nabla_\nu \equiv (\nabla, i\partial/c\partial t)$ the Lorentz condition becomes:

$$\nabla_\nu A_\nu = 0. \qquad [2.39]$$

Biot–Savart law

Since the vector potential $\mathbf{A}$ and the scalar potential ϕ are the components of the four-potential A_ν, many of the problems solved in electrostatics from Poisson's equation $\nabla^2 \phi = -\rho/\epsilon_0$ can be similarly solved in magnetostatics from the equation:

$$\nabla^2 \mathbf{A} = -\mu_0 \mathbf{j}. \qquad [2.40]$$

Thus equation [2.24] for ϕ becomes:

$$\mathbf{A}(1) = \frac{\mu_0}{4\pi} \int\limits_{\substack{\text{all} \\ \text{space}}} \frac{\mathbf{j}(2)\,d\tau_2}{r_{12}} \qquad [2.41]$$

for each component of the vector potential $\mathbf{A}(1)$ and the vector current density $\mathbf{j}(2)$, as in Fig. 2.8(a). Then we can find $\mathbf{B}(1)$ from:

$$\mathbf{B}(1) = \operatorname{curl} \mathbf{A}(1) = \operatorname{curl} \left\{ \frac{\mu_0}{4\pi} \int \frac{\mathbf{j}(2)\,d\tau_2}{r_{12}} \right\}$$

where:

$$r_{12}^2 = (x_1 - x_2)^2 + (y_1 - y_2)^2 + (z_1 - z_2)^2.$$

In finding the derivatives of $\mathbf{A}(1)$ we operate only on the $(x_1 y_1 z_1)$ coordinates, so that:

$$\begin{aligned}
B_x &= \frac{\partial A_z}{\partial y_1} - \frac{\partial A_y}{\partial z_1} = \frac{\mu_0}{4\pi} \int \left\{ j_z \frac{\partial}{\partial y_1}\left(\frac{1}{r_{12}}\right) - j_y \frac{\partial}{\partial z_1}\left(\frac{1}{r_{12}}\right) \right\} d\tau_2 \\
&= \frac{\mu_0}{4\pi} \int \left\{ \frac{-j_z(y_1 - y_2)}{r_{12}^3} + \frac{j_y(z_1 - z_2)}{r_{12}^3} \right\} d\tau_2.
\end{aligned}$$

Here the integrand is just the x component of $(\mathbf{j} \times \mathbf{r}_{12})/r_{12}^3$ and, by symmetry, we therefore find:

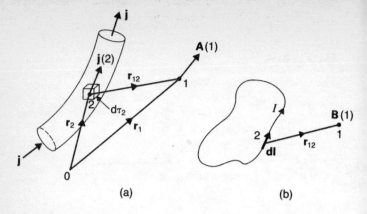

Fig. 2.8 (a) Vector potential **A**(1) for a distribution of current density **j**. (b) Magnetic field **B**(1) due to a current I

$$\mathbf{B}(1) = \frac{\mu_0}{4\pi} \int\limits_{\substack{\text{all} \\ \text{space}}} \frac{\mathbf{j}(2) \times \mathbf{r}_{12}}{r_{12}^3} \, d\tau_2. \qquad [2.42]$$

In many circuits the current is carried in wires whose diameters are very small compared with the other dimensions of the circuit. For thin wires the volume element $d\tau = S\,dl$ and the current density **j** is along **dl** and uniform over S, so that:

$$\mathbf{j}\,d\tau = \mathbf{j}S\,dl = I\mathbf{dl} \qquad [2.43]$$

where I is the current in the circuit. Then equation [2.42] becomes:

$$\mathbf{B}(1) = \frac{\mu_0}{4\pi} \oint \frac{I\mathbf{dl} \times \mathbf{r}_{12}}{r_{12}^3} \qquad [2.44]$$

where the integration is taken all round the circuit (Fig. 2.8(b)). This is the law of Biot and Savart for steady currents.

2.4 Energy of electromagnetic field

We consider here the energy that arises from fixed charges electrostatically and from steady currents magnetostatically. Later we shall consider the energy density under dynamic conditions such as that carried by an electromagnetic wave.

Electrostatic energy

The potential energy of an infinitesimal volume of charge $\rho \, d\tau$ is the product $\rho \phi \, d\tau$, where ϕ is the potential due to any other charges (Fig. 2.9). To find the total electrostatic energy U we

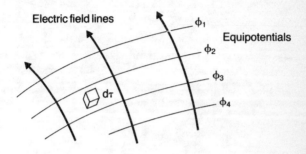

Fig. 2.9 Equipotentials in an electric field

must integrate this over the charge distribution, remembering that such an integral would count all the pairs $\rho_i \phi_i \, d\tau$ twice. Therefore:

$$U = \frac{1}{2} \int_\tau \rho \phi \, d\tau. \qquad [2.45]$$

This expression is adequate for a distribution of fixed charges, but if we integrate it using Poisson's equation $\nabla^2 \phi = -\rho/\epsilon_0$, we can obtain a more general result in terms of the electric field **E**. We have:

$$U = -\frac{\epsilon_0}{2} \int_\tau \phi \nabla^2 \phi \, d\tau$$

or

$$U = -\frac{\epsilon_0}{2} \int_\tau (\phi \nabla \cdot \nabla \phi) \, d\tau.$$

Using the vector identity for div ΩA, where Ω and A are arbitrary scalar and vector functions (Appendix 4, equation [A4.1]), this becomes:

$$U = -\frac{\epsilon_0}{2}\int_\tau \nabla.(\phi \, \nabla\phi)\mathrm{d}\tau + \frac{\epsilon_0}{2}\int_\tau \nabla\phi.\nabla\phi \, \mathrm{d}\tau.$$

Applying Gauss's divergence theorem (equation [A4.19]) to the first integral:

$$U = -\frac{\epsilon_0}{2}\int_S (\phi \, \nabla\phi).\mathrm{d}S + \frac{\epsilon_0}{2}\int_\tau E.E\mathrm{d}\tau.$$

For a finite volume τ of charges, the surface S can be made as large as we wish. The integrand is the product $\phi\nabla\phi$, which must decrease at least as fast as $1/r \times 1/r^2 = 1/r^3$, whereas the surface area of S will increase only as r^2. Thus this contribution to the potential energy is negligible and

$$U = \frac{\epsilon_0}{2}\int_\tau E.E\mathrm{d}\tau. \qquad [2.46]$$

An energy density $u = U/\tau$ in the electrostatic field (Fig. 2.9) of $\frac{1}{2}\,\epsilon_0 E^2$ would produce the same total energy U and this interpretation of the electric energy is particularly useful for electromagnetism. On the other hand, it is only for fixed charges that one can write equation [2.45].

Magnetostatic energy

In establishing a distribution of steady currents there is an initial transient period when the currents and their associated fields are brought from zero to their final values. During this period there are time-dependent fields which induce electromotive forces, and so the total magnetic energy of steady currents must include work done in establishing those currents. For a single circuit carrying current I, if the magnetic flux Φ through it changes, then an e.m.f. $\mathcal{E}$ is induced around it. In order to keep the current I constant, the batteries must do work at the rate:

$$\frac{\mathrm{d}U}{\mathrm{d}t} = -I\mathcal{E} = \frac{I\mathrm{d}\Phi}{\mathrm{d}t}$$

from Faraday's law. Such a circuit can be considered to be composed of a large number of current loops (Fig. 2.10), each of which carries the current I around an infinitesimal area $\mathrm{d}S$ with normal $\mathbf{dS}$. An increment of work $\mathrm{d}U$ done against the induced e.m.f. in the loop is given by the change in the magnetic field $\mathbf{dB}$ through the loop:

$$\mathrm{d}U = I\mathbf{dS}.\mathbf{dB}.$$

The total energy in establishing the magnetic field $\mathbf{B}$ of all the loops is then:

$$U = I\int_S \mathbf{B}.\mathbf{dS} \qquad [2.47]$$

and expressing $\mathbf{B}$ in terms of the vector potential:

$$U = I\int_S (\mathrm{curl}\ \mathbf{A}).\mathbf{dS}.$$

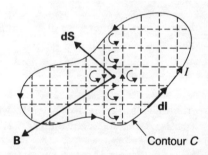

Fig. 2.10 A circuit carrying a current I is equivalent to a large number of current loops of magnetic dipole moment $I\mathbf{dS}$ and this can be used to find the magnetic energy of the circuit in a magnetic field $\mathbf{B}$

By Stokes's theorem (Appendix 4) this integral over the total surface S of the circuit can be expressed in terms of its contour C by:

$$U = I\oint_C \mathbf{A}.\mathbf{dl}. \qquad [2.48]$$

The thin wires of the circuit can be replaced by current filaments, such that:

$$I\mathbf{dl} = \mathbf{j}d\tau \qquad\qquad [2.43]$$

and for each pair of such circuits the magnetic energy is given by equations [2.48], where the integral is over the volume of the current filaments of one circuit and the vector potential is due to the other circuit. For the total energy if we take the sum over all filaments we should be counting each filament twice so that, like equation [2.45], we obtain:

$$U = \frac{1}{2}\int_{\tau} \mathbf{j}.\mathbf{A}d\tau. \qquad\qquad [2.49]$$

This expression is adequate for a distribution of steady currents, but if we interpret it using Ampère's law in differential form,

$$\text{curl } \mathbf{B} = \mu_0\mathbf{j}, \qquad\qquad [2.50]$$

we can obtain a more general result in terms of the magnetic field $\mathbf{B}$. Hence:

$$U = \frac{1}{2}\mu_0\int_{\tau} (\text{curl } \mathbf{B}).\mathbf{A}d\tau.$$

Using the vector identity for div $(\mathbf{A} \times \mathbf{B})$, where $\mathbf{A}$ and $\mathbf{B}$ are arbitrary vectors (Appendix 4, equation [A4.2]), this becomes:

$$U = \frac{1}{2}\mu_0\int_{\tau} \{ \mathbf{B}.\text{curl } \mathbf{A} - \text{div } (\mathbf{A} \times \mathbf{B}) \} \ d\tau.$$

Applying Gauss's divergence theorem (equation [A4.19]) to the second term, this becomes:

$$U = \frac{1}{2}\mu_0\int_{\tau} \mathbf{B}.\mathbf{B}d\tau - \frac{1}{2}\mu_0\int_{S} (\mathbf{A} \times \mathbf{B}).\mathbf{dS}.$$

For a finite system of currents, the surface S can be made as large as we wish. The integral over a surface a long way from the system would vanish, since $\mathbf{A} \times \mathbf{B}$ falls off at least as fast as r^{-3}, while S increases only as r^2. Hence the total magnetic energy of a system of steady currents in conductors is:

$$U = \frac{\mu_0}{2} \int_\tau \mathbf{B}.\mathbf{B} d\tau. \qquad [2.51]$$

As with the electrostatic field, an energy density $u = U/\tau$ in the magnetostatic field of $\frac{1}{2} \mu_0 B^2$ would produce the same total energy U and this interpretation is particularly useful in electromagnetism. On the other hand it is only for a system of steady currents that one can use equation [2.49].

2.5 Retarded potentials

We have shown that Maxwell's four equations for the $\mathbf{E}$ and $\mathbf{B}$ fields (equations [1.1] to [1.4]) are equivalent to one four-vector equation:

$$\square A_\nu = -\mu_0 j_\nu \qquad [2.38]$$

provided we choose the Lorentz gauge for A_ν:

$$\nabla_\nu A_\nu = 0. \qquad [2.39]$$

Here A_ν was the four-vector $(\mathbf{A}, i\phi/c)$, so that equation [2.38] is a set of three equations for the components of $\mathbf{A}$ and an equation for ϕ:

$$\nabla^2 \mathbf{A} - \frac{1}{c^2} \frac{\partial^2 \mathbf{A}}{\partial t^2} = -\mu_0 \mathbf{j} \qquad [2.33]$$

$$\nabla^2 \phi - \frac{1}{c^2} \frac{\partial^2 \phi}{\partial t^2} = -\rho/\epsilon_0. \qquad [2.32]$$

For a distribution of charges and currents (Fig. 2.11) we can integrate these *inhomogeneous wave equations* in a similar way to the integration of Poisson's equation, $\nabla^2 \phi = -\rho/\epsilon_0$, which yields the familiar scalar potential:

$$\phi(1) = \frac{1}{4\pi\epsilon_0} \int \frac{\rho(2)}{r_{12}} d\tau_2. \qquad [2.52]$$

The difference, now that we have moving charges, from the electrostatic result is that the potentials at the fixed field points $[1, t] = (x_1 y_1 z_1 t)$ are due to the charges and currents at the source points at the earlier time $(t - r_{12}/c)$ to allow for the

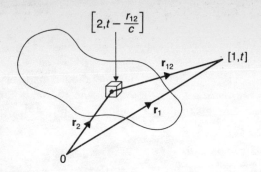

Fig. 2.11 The retarded potentials at point [1, t] are calculated from integrals of the charge density and current density at source points [2, t − r_{12}/c] within a source distribution

fields to propagate at the finite speed c.

The solutions of equations [2.33] and [2.32] are therefore the retarded vector and scalar potentials:

$$\mathbf{A}(1, t) = \frac{\mu_0}{4\pi} \int \frac{\mathbf{j}(2, t - r_{12}/c)}{r_{12}} \, d\tau_2 \qquad [2.53]$$

$$\phi(1, t) = \frac{1}{4\pi\epsilon_0} \int \frac{\rho(2, t - r_{12}/c)}{r_{12}} \, d\tau_2. \qquad [2.54]$$

These potentials replace the static potentials of equations [2.41] and [2.52] whenever we are not dealing with the separate electrostatic ($\partial \mathbf{E}/\partial t = 0$) or magnetostatic ($\partial \mathbf{B}/\partial t = 0$) solutions of Maxwell's equations. They show clearly the relativistic nature of the electromagnetic field and the speed of propagation of electromagnetism in space. They are expressed in the four-vector notation by:

$$A_\nu(1, t) = \frac{\mu_0}{4\pi} \int \frac{j_\nu(2, t - r_{12}/c)}{r_{12}} \, d\tau_2. \qquad [2.55]$$

Chapter 3
Electromagnetic waves in space

Electromagnetic fields propagate in space, in dielectrics and, to a limited extent, in plasmas and conductors. The basic properties of electromagnetic waves are revealed by studying their propagation in space, so we begin by solving Maxwell's equations in free space for their wave solutions and then determine the flow of energy in these waves.

3.1 Wave equations

In empty space there can be no electric charges or currents, so Maxwell's equations become:

$$\text{div } \mathbf{E} = 0 \qquad\qquad\qquad [1.5]$$

$$\text{div } \mathbf{B} = 0 \qquad\qquad\qquad [1.6]$$

$$\text{curl } \mathbf{E} = - \partial \mathbf{B}/\partial t \qquad\qquad [1.7]$$

$$\text{curl } \mathbf{B} = \mu_0 \epsilon_0 \ \partial \mathbf{E}/\partial t. \qquad\qquad [1.8]$$

By taking the curl of equations [1.7] and [1.8] and using the vector identity for curl $\mathbf{A}$, where $\mathbf{A}$ is any vector (Appendix 4, equation [A4.6]) we obtain:

$$\text{grad div } \mathbf{E} - \nabla^2 \mathbf{E} = - \text{curl } (\partial \mathbf{B}/\partial t) = -\frac{\partial}{\partial t}(\text{curl } \mathbf{B})$$

$$\text{grad div } \mathbf{B} - \nabla^2 \mathbf{B} = \mu_0 \epsilon_0 \text{ curl } (\partial \mathbf{E}/\partial t) = \mu_0 \epsilon_0 \frac{\partial}{\partial t}(\text{curl } \mathbf{E})$$

since the space operators are independent of the time coordinates.

Remembering equations [1.5], [1.6] and re-using [1.7] and [1.8], these become:

$$\nabla^2 \mathbf{E} = \mu_0 \epsilon_0 \, \partial^2 \mathbf{E}/\partial t^2 \qquad\qquad [3.1]$$

$$\nabla^2 \mathbf{B} = \mu_0 \epsilon_0 \, \partial^2 \mathbf{B}/\partial t^2 . \qquad\qquad [3.2]$$

The electric constant ϵ_0 is defined as $1/(\mu_0 c^2)$, so that equations [3.1] and [3.2] are:

$$\nabla^2 \mathbf{E} - \frac{1}{c^2} \frac{\partial^2 \mathbf{E}}{\partial t^2} = 0 \qquad\qquad [3.3]$$

$$\nabla^2 \mathbf{B} - \frac{1}{c^2} \frac{\partial^2 \mathbf{B}}{\partial t^2} = 0. \qquad\qquad [3.4]$$

We thus have the remarkable result that, in space, the electric field $\mathbf{E}\,(\mathbf{r}, t)$, the magnetic field $\mathbf{B}\,(\mathbf{r}, t)$, the scalar potential $\phi\,(\mathbf{r}, t)$ and the vector potential $\mathbf{A}\,(\mathbf{r}, t)$, from equations [3.2], [3.4], [2.32] and [2.33], all satisfy the same basic, four-dimensional wave equation:

$$\nabla^2 \psi = \frac{1}{c^2} \frac{\partial^2 \psi}{\partial t^2} . \qquad\qquad [3.5]$$

This equation is well known and its general solution is a super-position of an infinite set of one-dimensional waves travelling in all possible directions. We can therefore obtain the basic information we need by studying the equation for one spatial dimension and the time:

$$\frac{\partial^2 \psi}{\partial z^2} = \frac{1}{c^2} \frac{\partial^2 \psi}{\partial t^2} . \qquad\qquad [3.6]$$

Let us suppose that at $t = 0$ the solution is an arbitrary function, $f\,(z)$, as shown in Fig. 3.1. It travels along $0z$ at speed c, so that at time t it has travelled a distance ct and in space it will not be distorted. The solution is therefore of the form:

$$\psi = f\,(z - ct) \qquad\qquad [3.7]$$

which the reader can readily see satisfies equation [3.6] by partial differentiation. It is also possible for the wave to be travelling at speed c in the opposite direction, $- z$. A general solution of

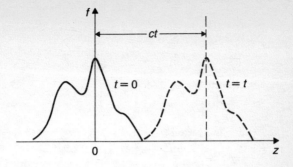

Fig. 3.1 A plane wave ψ (z, t) travelling along $0z$ at speed c in the time t

equation [3.6] is therefore:

$$\psi = f(z - ct) + g(z + ct).$$ [3.8]

There is no need to introduce a particular frequency into this general solution, as there is no dispersion for electromagnetic waves in space. All such waves, from the highest-frequency cosmic rays (see electromagnetic spectrum) to the lowest-frequency radio waves, travel in space at exactly the same speed, c. This has been verified over many years in numerous precision experiments, notably those with monochromatic light and microwaves. The accepted value for c from these experiments, to an accuracy of 4 parts in 10^9, is:

$$c = 299\ 792\ 458 \text{ m s}^{-1}.$$ [3.9]

However, the SI base units of length and time are now defined in terms of the wavelength λ of a transition of the ^{86}Kr atom (1 m = 1 650 763.73 λ) and the frequency ν of a transition of the ^{133}Cs atom (1 s = 9 192 631 770 ν^{-1}). Since the radiation from each of these transitions travels at speed c, a measurement of c is now directly related to these transitions. For problems it is usually acceptable to take $c = 3.00 \times 10^8$ m s^{-1}.

3.2 Plane waves

The simplest waves are plane waves, i.e. waves where the fields are constant in a plane (say, xy) at an instant in time for a wave propagating along an axis normal to the plane (say, z). The electric field, for example, in a plane electromagnetic wave is given by the real part of:

$$\mathbf{E} = \mathbf{E_0} \exp i \left(\omega t - kz \right) \tag{3.10}$$

where the time-period $T = 2\pi/\omega$, the wavelength $\lambda = 2\pi/k$ and the phase velocity $\omega/k = c$ (Fig. 3.2). (It is conventional in electromagnetism and optics to write a wavefunction in this way with $+ i\omega t$, although in quantum mechanics and solid state physics the opposite convention of $- i\omega t$ is usual.)

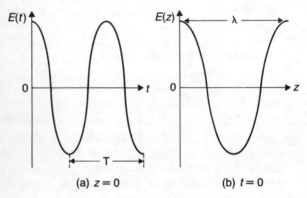

(a) $z = 0$ (b) $t = 0$

Fig. 3.2 A plane wave $E(z, t)$ has a time period T when observed (a) at $z = 0$ and a wavelength λ measured (b) at $t = 0$ along $0z$

In our plane wave at a fixed time (Fig. 3.2(b)) the field vector $\mathbf{E}$ is constant in the xy plane, so that:

$$\frac{\partial E_x}{\partial x} = \frac{\partial E_y}{\partial y} = 0. \tag{3.11}$$

But the wave must satisfy Maxwell's first equation [1.5]

$$\frac{\partial E_x}{\partial x} + \frac{\partial E_y}{\partial y} + \frac{\partial E_z}{\partial z} = 0. \tag{3.12}$$

Combining equations [3.11] and [3.12], we have:

$$\frac{\partial E_z}{\partial z} = 0 \qquad [3.13]$$

or E_z is constant. However, from equation [3.10]:

$$\frac{\partial \mathbf{E}}{\partial z} = -k\mathbf{E} \qquad [3.14]$$

and the only value of E_z that will satisfy both [3.13] and [3.14] is:

$$E_z = 0.$$

Therefore $\mathbf{E_0}$ is a vector in the xy plane normal to the direction of propagation $0z$.

In a similar way the magnetic field in a plane electromagnetic wave is given by the real part of:

$$\mathbf{B} = \mathbf{B_0} \exp i\,(\omega t - kz). \qquad [3.15]$$

Since $\mathbf{B}$ must satisfy Maxwell's second equation [1.6],

$$\text{div } \mathbf{B} = 0$$

a similar argument shows that $B_z = 0$ and therefore $\mathbf{B_0}$ is also a vector in the xy plane. Of course, $\mathbf{E}$ and $\mathbf{B}$ are related in Maxwell's third and fourth equations, so there must be a relationship between $\mathbf{E_0}$ and $\mathbf{B_0}$ in an electromagnetic wave. To find this, let

$$\mathbf{E_0} = E_{0x}\,\hat{\mathbf{i}} + E_{0y}\,\hat{\mathbf{j}} \qquad [3.16]$$

where E_{0x}, E_{0y} are constants and $\hat{\mathbf{i}}, \hat{\mathbf{j}}$ are unit vectors. Substituting [3.10] and [3.16] in Maxwell's third equation [1.7] we have:

$$\text{curl } \left\{ (E_{0x}\,\hat{\mathbf{i}} + E_{0y}\,\hat{\mathbf{j}}) \exp i\,(\omega t - kz) \right\} = -\frac{\partial \mathbf{B}}{\partial t}. \qquad [3.17]$$

The only components of curl $\mathbf{E}$ that are finite are $\partial E_x/\partial z$ and $\partial E_y/\partial z$, so that [3.17] becomes:

$$(-ik\,E_{0x}\,\hat{\mathbf{j}} + ik\,E_{0y}\,\hat{\mathbf{i}}) \exp i\,(\omega t - kz) = -\,\partial \mathbf{B}/\partial t.$$

If we now integrate to find $\mathbf{B}$ and take it to be entirely oscillatory, we divide by $i\omega$ and get:

$$\frac{k}{\omega} E_{0x} \, \hat{\mathbf{j}} - \frac{k}{\omega} E_{0y} \, \hat{\mathbf{i}} = \mathbf{B}_0.$$

However, $c = \omega/k$ is the phase velocity and so the vector $\mathbf{B}$ is just:

$$\mathbf{B} = \frac{1}{c}(\hat{\mathbf{k}} \times \mathbf{E}). \qquad [3.18]$$

This shows that $\mathbf{B}$ is normal to both $\mathbf{E}$ and the direction of propagation $(\hat{\mathbf{k}})$ and similarly for $\mathbf{E}$. Electromagnetic waves are therefore *transverse waves*. The relative directions of $\mathbf{E}$ and $\mathbf{B}$ are shown in Fig. 3.3 for waves travelling along $+ z$ and $- z$. Of course, the amplitude of $\mathbf{B}$ is very small; for example, 1 kV m^{-1} for E corresponds to only $3.3 \, \mu\text{T}$ for B.

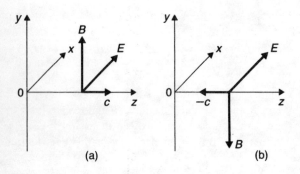

Fig. 3.3 A plane electromagnetic wave travelling (a) in the $+ z$ direction and (b) in the $- z$ direction

Polarisation

The plane wave described by equation [3.16] is said to be *linearly* polarised, because the electric field exists in one transverse direction only as it propagates (Fig. 3.4(a)), given by:

$$\tan \theta = \frac{E_{0y}}{E_{0x}} . \qquad [3.19]$$

In this case the x and y components of $\mathbf{E_0}$ can be of different magnitudes but they are always in phase and so θ is a constant.

A plane wave composed of x and y components that have a constant phase difference, as well as different amplitudes, is *elliptically* polarised; a special case is when the amplitudes are the same and the wave is then said to be *circularly* polarised. In general, then:

$$\mathbf{E} = E_{0x}\,\hat{\mathbf{i}}\exp i\,(\omega t - kz + \phi_x) + E_{0y}\,\hat{\mathbf{j}}\exp i\,(\omega t - kz + \phi_y)$$

and if $\phi_y - \phi_x = \pi/2$, the real part is:

$$\mathbf{E} = E_{0x}\,\hat{\mathbf{i}}\cos\,(\omega t - kz + \phi_x) - E_{0y}\,\hat{\mathbf{j}}\sin\,(\omega t - kx + \phi_x).$$

Thus $\mathbf{E}$ rotates in the xy plane with direction:

$$\tan\,(\omega t - kz + \phi_x) = -\frac{E_{0y}}{E_{0x}} \qquad [3.20]$$

which traces out a circle when $E_{0x} = E_{0y}$ (Fig. 3.4(b)) and an ellipse when $E_{0x} \neq E_{0y}$ (Fig. 3.4(c)).

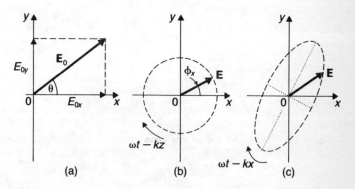

Fig. 3.4 The electric vector in a plane wave that is (a) linearly polarised, (b) circularly polarised and (c) elliptically polarised

The direction of rotation is defined as *right-handed* when, on looking into the wave along the direction of propagation, the electric vector is rotating counter-clockwise. The waves shown in Fig. 3.4(b) and (c) are thus *left-handed* polarisations. These definitions are the ones used in modern optics and in particle physics, the right-handed photon having positive helicity and spin vector in the direction of motion. (In classical optics the opposite convention was used.)

3.3 Spherical waves

Plane waves are the simplest to describe mathematically and will be used extensively to study propagation in dielectrics and conductors in later chapters. In free space they propagate without any decrease in amplitude, unlike the waves from a point source or dipole, which spread out like the ripples from a stone thrown into a lake. In three dimensions such waves are spherical waves and it is instructive to rewrite the wave equation [3.5] in spherical polar coordinates and consider its spherically symmetric solution.

The Laplacian in spherical polars with spherical symmetry is (Appendix 4):

$$\nabla^2 \psi = \frac{1}{r^2} \frac{\partial}{\partial r} \left(r^2 \frac{\partial \psi}{\partial r} \right) \qquad [3.21]$$

or

$$\nabla^2 \psi = \frac{1}{r^2} \left\{ 2r \frac{\partial \psi}{\partial r} + r^2 \frac{\partial^2 \psi}{\partial r^2} \right\}.$$

It is easily seen that this can be written:

$$\nabla^2 \psi = \frac{1}{r} \left\{ \frac{\partial^2}{\partial r^2} (r\psi) \right\}$$

so that equation [3.5] becomes:

$$\frac{1}{r} \frac{\partial^2}{\partial r^2} (r\psi) = \frac{1}{c^2} \frac{\partial^2}{\partial t^2} (\psi) \qquad [3.22]$$

or

$$\frac{\partial^2}{\partial r^2} (r\psi) = \frac{1}{c^2} \frac{\partial^2}{\partial t^2} (r\psi).$$

The solution is therefore of the same form as equation [3.7]:

$$r\psi\,(r,\,t) = f\,(r-ct)$$

or

$$\psi\,(r,\,t) = \frac{1}{r} f\,(r-ct).\qquad\qquad [3.23]$$

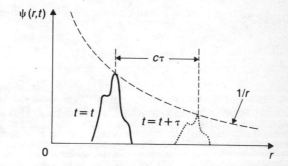

Fig. 3.5 A spherical wave $\psi\,(r,\,t)$ travelling along 0r at speed c decays in amplitude as $1/r$

Thus a spherical wave decays in amplitude as $1/r$ (Fig. 3.5), unlike the constant amplitude plane wave (Fig. 3.1). There are two other ways in which these waves differ. First, it is obvious that the solution (equation [3.23]) cannot apply at the origin, $r = 0$, where the amplitude would be infinite. We shall see in Chapter 7, when we discuss the generation of electromagnetic waves, that the spherical wave solution is not valid when $r \ll \lambda$, the wavelength of the wave. Secondly, the solution which we found for the plane wave travelling in the opposite direction:

$$\psi\,(r,\,t) = \frac{1}{r} g\,(r+ct)\qquad\qquad [3.24]$$

also satisfies equation [3.22], but implies a spherical wave collapsing to a source point. This is a valid solution of Maxwell's equations for waves from a spherical reflector but, like the outward solution (equation [3.23]), the inward solution (equation [3.24]) is not valid near the origin when $r \ll \lambda$.

3.4 Energy density and energy flow

An important principle in electromagnetism is the conservation of electric charge. It is recognised as of similar validity to the conservation of energy. In this section we consider the application of these conservation principles to the production and flow of energy in electromagnetic waves in space.

An electric current I is the current density flux from a surface S given by:

$$I = \int_S \mathbf{j}.\mathbf{dS} = \int \frac{\mathrm{d}q}{\mathrm{d}t} \qquad [3.25]$$

where q is the charge flowing out of the surface S and equation [3.25] shows that electric charge is conserved. If S is a closed surface enclosing a volume V of charge density ρ then, using Gauss's divergence theorem (Appendix 4), we can write:

$$\int_V \mathrm{div}\,\mathbf{j}\,\mathrm{d}\tau = -\frac{\mathrm{d}}{\mathrm{d}t}\left(\int_V \rho\mathrm{d}\tau \right).$$

Hence, for a small volume $\mathrm{d}\tau$, we obtain a local conservation of electric charge, the *equation of continuity*:

$$\mathrm{div}\,\mathbf{j} = -\frac{\partial \rho}{\partial t}. \qquad [3.26]$$

This equation shows that the flux of charge density flowing out of the volume $\mathrm{d}\tau$ is just equal to the rate of loss of charge density inside that volume. A similar conservation principle must apply to the energy flow into and out of a small volume, but now the charges are accelerated by an electric field $\mathbf{E}$ in order to produce an electromagnetic energy flux $\mathscr{S}$.

The rate of doing work on an electric charge q moving at velocity $\mathbf{v}$ is, by the Lorentz force law equation [2.10]:

$$\mathbf{F}.\mathbf{v} = q\,\mathbf{E}.\mathbf{v}$$

or for a volume $\mathrm{d}\tau$:

$$q\,\mathbf{E}.\mathbf{v} = \rho\mathrm{d}\tau\,\mathbf{E}.\mathbf{v} = \mathbf{E}.\mathbf{j}\,\mathrm{d}\tau.$$

If the energy density in space is u, then the rate of loss of energy density from any volume V must equal the flow of energy out of the surface S of that volume plus the rate of doing work on the moving charges in V that generates the energy flow, or:

$$-\frac{\partial}{\partial t}\left(\int_V u\,d\tau\right) = \int_S \mathscr{S}.\mathbf{dS} + \int_V \mathbf{E}.\mathbf{j}\,d\tau.$$

Applying Gauss's divergence theorem to the flux of $\mathscr{S}$, we obtain a similar equation to the equation of continuity, that is:

$$-\frac{\partial u}{\partial t} = \operatorname{div}\mathscr{S} + \mathbf{E}.\mathbf{j} \qquad [3.27]$$

the *equation of conservation of energy flow*.

In 1884 Poynting solved this equation, using Maxwell's equations, to find the flux $\mathscr{S}$, which is now known as the Poynting vector, and the energy density u. We want to eliminate $\mathbf{j}$, and find $\mathscr{S}$ and u in terms of the electric $\mathbf{E}$ and magnetic $\mathbf{B}$ fields. Substituting for $\mathbf{j}$ from equation [1.4], we obtain:

$$\mathbf{E}.\mathbf{j} = \mathbf{E}.\left(\operatorname{curl}\frac{\mathbf{B}}{\mu_0}\right) - \epsilon_0\,\mathbf{E}.\frac{\partial \mathbf{E}}{\partial t}. \qquad [3.28]$$

We recognise the second term as $\partial u/\partial t$ for the electric vector, from equation [2.46], and expect the first term to contain $\partial u/\partial t$ for the magnetic vector, from equation [2.51]. Using the vector identity for div $(\mathbf{A} \times \mathbf{B})$ from Appendix 4, the first term becomes:

$$\mathbf{E}.\left(\operatorname{curl}\frac{\mathbf{B}}{\mu_0}\right) = \operatorname{div}\left(\frac{\mathbf{B}}{\mu_0} \times \mathbf{E}\right) + \frac{\mathbf{B}}{\mu_0}.(\operatorname{curl}\mathbf{E}). \qquad [3.29]$$

Now, using Maxwell's equation [1.3], we see that the last term is:

$$\frac{\mathbf{B}}{\mu_0}.\left(-\frac{\partial \mathbf{B}}{\partial t}\right) = -\frac{\partial}{\partial t}\left(\frac{\mathbf{B}.\mathbf{B}}{2\mu_0}\right) \qquad [3.30]$$

and substituting from equations [3.29] and [3.30] in [3.28], we have:

$$\mathbf{E}.\mathbf{j} = \operatorname{div}\left(\frac{\mathbf{B}}{\mu_0} \times \mathbf{E}\right) - \frac{\partial}{\partial t}\left\{\frac{\mathbf{B}.\mathbf{B}}{2\mu_0} + \frac{\epsilon_0\,\mathbf{E}.\mathbf{E}}{2}\right\}.$$

Comparing this equation with equation [3.27], we find Poynting's solutions for $\mathscr{S}$ and u for energy flow in free space:

$$\mathscr{S} = \mathbf{E} \times \frac{\mathbf{B}}{\mu_0} \equiv \mathbf{E} \times \mathbf{H} \qquad [3.31]$$

$$u = \frac{1}{2} \left\{ \frac{\mathbf{B}}{\mu_0} . \mathbf{B} + \epsilon_0\, \mathbf{E} . \mathbf{E} \right\}. \qquad [3.32]$$

Poynting vector

We have seen that a plane electromagnetic wave in space with its electric vector along $\hat{\mathbf{i}}$ and its magnetic vector along $\hat{\mathbf{j}}$ (Fig. 3.3(a)) can be described by:

$$\mathbf{E} = E_{0x}\, \exp i\,(\omega t - kz)\, \hat{\mathbf{i}} \qquad [3.33]$$

and

$$\mathbf{B} = \frac{1}{c}(\hat{\mathbf{k}} \times \mathbf{E}) = \frac{E_{0x}}{c}\, \exp i\,(\omega t - kz)\, \hat{\mathbf{j}}. \qquad [3.34]$$

For this wave the Poynting vector is:

$$\mathscr{S} = \mathbf{E} \times \frac{\mathbf{B}}{\mu_0} = \frac{\mathbf{E} \times (\hat{\mathbf{k}} \times \mathbf{E})}{c\mu_0} = \epsilon_0 c E^2 \hat{\mathbf{k}}. \qquad [3.35]$$

This is the instantaneous rate of flow of energy across unit area, which is normally averaged over time to produce the intensity of the waves:

$\mu_0 = 4\pi \times 10^{-7} N/amp$

$$\langle \mathscr{S} \rangle = \epsilon_0 c \langle E^2 \rangle. \qquad [3.36]$$

For example, a radio wave with $E = 0.1$ V m^{-1} has an intensity of $10^{-2}/(4\pi \times 10^{-7} \times 3 \times 10^8) = 30\ \mu\text{W m}^{-2}$.

The intensity can also be computed from the fluctuating fields through the energy density u (equation [3.32]). The plane wave of equations [3.33] and [3.34] is shown diagrammatically in Fig. 3.6(a), $\mathbf{E}$ oscillating in the xz plane and $\mathbf{B}$ in the yz plane. Although the mean values of $\mathbf{E}$ and $\mathbf{B}$ are zero, the average of the energy density:

$$u = \frac{1}{2} \frac{E^2}{\mu_0 c^2} + \frac{1}{2} \epsilon_0 E^2 \qquad [3.37]$$

$\mu_0 \epsilon_0 = \dfrac{1}{c^2}$

$\epsilon_0 c = \dfrac{1}{\mu_0 c}$

is not zero but:

$$\langle u \rangle = \epsilon_0 \langle E^2 \rangle$$

since $\epsilon_0 = 1/(\mu_0 c^2)$ and the electric and magnetic energies are equal for an electromagnetic plane wave in space. The wave is travelling at speed c and so, from Fig. 3.6(b), the mean energy flow is just the mean energy in a box length c and cross-section 1 m^2, or:

$$\langle \mathscr{S} \rangle = (\epsilon_0 \langle E^2 \rangle)c$$

as before.

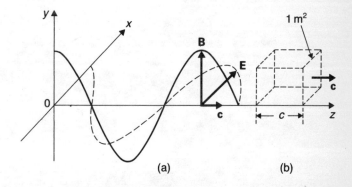

Fig. 3.6 (a) A plane electromagnetic wave travelling along $0z$ with electric vector in the xz, and magnetic vector in the yz, planes. (b) The mean energy flow in the wave is the energy density in the box length c, cross-sectional area 1 m^2

In free space $\mathscr{S}$ is given both by $(\mathbf{E} \times \mathbf{B}/\mu_0)$ and $(\mathbf{E} \times \mathbf{H})$. It is not clear from this as to whether $\mathscr{S}$ in a magnetisable medium would be $(\mathbf{E} \times \mathbf{B}/\mu_0)$, where $\mathbf{B}/\mu_0 = \mathbf{H} + \mathbf{M}$, or $(\mathbf{E} \times \mathbf{H})$. We shall discuss this when we consider propagation in matter.

When considering the flow of electromagnetic energy between two media (Chapter 4) a useful parameter is found to be that of *wave impedance*, Z. This is defined for free space by:

$$Z_0 = \frac{E_{0x}}{H_{0y}} = \frac{\mu E_{0x}}{B_{0y}} \qquad [3.38]$$

which with equation [3.33] and [3.34] gives:

$$Z_0 = \mu_0 c. \qquad [3.39]$$

Since E is measured in $V\,m^{-1}$ and H in $A\,m^{-1}$, the wave impedance has the same dimensions as a circuit impedance, and from [3.39]:

$$Z_0 = 377 \text{ ohm.} \qquad [3.40]$$

Chapter 4
Electromagnetic waves in dielectrics

Consideration of the propagation of electromagnetic waves in matter can be conveniently divided into two cases: (1) dielectrics, i.e. media in which there are no conduction electrons, and (2) conductors. Many gases, liquids and solids are good dielectrics and we begin with the effects of an oscillating electric field on such dielectrics. We then solve Maxwell's equations for linear, isotropic dielectrics and finally discuss the absorption and dispersion of electromagnetic waves in polar and non-polar dielectrics.

4.1 Polarisation of dielectrics

In electrostatics an applied electric field $\mathbf{E}$ produces polarisation charges in dielectric media and a polarisation $\mathbf{P}$ (equation [1.13]) related to the electric field by:

$$\mathbf{P} = \epsilon_0 \chi_e \mathbf{E} \qquad [4.1]$$

where $\chi_e = (\epsilon_r - 1)$ is the electric susceptibility of the dielectric and ϵ_0 is inserted to make χ_e dimensionless. The polarisation of a dielectric is defined in terms of its internal dipole moments $\mathbf{p}$ by:

$$\mathbf{P} = N\mathbf{p} \qquad [4.2]$$

when there are N dipoles per unit volume. For a non-polar gas these dipole moments will be induced by the applied electric field and the *polarisability* α of the gas is given by:

$$\mathbf{p} = \alpha \mathbf{E}. \qquad [4.3]$$

A simple atomic model for such a gas is that of electrons bound to their nuclei such that any displacement by an applied electric field is balanced by a restoring force proportional to that displacement.

For this model, application of a linearly polarised electromagnetic wave with electric vector of magnitude

$$E_x = E_0 \exp(i\omega t) \tag{4.4}$$

would induce a damped, simple harmonic motion in the bound electrons given by

$$-eE_x = m(\ddot{x} + \gamma\dot{x} + \omega_0{}^2 x) \tag{4.5}$$

where x is the displacement parallel to E_x, γ is the damping constant of the electronic oscillators of natural frequency ω_0 and the effect of the magnetic component of the electromagnetic wave is assumed to be negligible. The steady-state displacements will be the dynamic responses to the incident wave, after initial transients:

$$x = x_0 \exp(i\omega t)$$

and so

$$\dot{x} = i\omega x, \quad \ddot{x} = -\omega^2 x.$$

Hence:

$$\mathbf{x} = \frac{-e}{m(\omega_0{}^2 - \omega^2 + i\gamma\omega)} \mathbf{E}. \tag{4.6}$$

The instantaneous dipole moment due to the displacement of the electron is

$$\mathbf{p} = -e\mathbf{x} \tag{4.7}$$

so that combining equations [4.6] and [4.7] and comparing with equation [4.3], we have the polarisability

$$\alpha(\omega) = \frac{e^2}{m(\omega_0{}^2 - \omega^2 + i\gamma\omega)}. \tag{4.8}$$

Clearly the polarisability is now a frequency-dependent parameter, and equations [4.2], [4.3] show that the polarisation is

$$\mathbf{P} = N\alpha(\omega)\mathbf{E}. \tag{4.9}$$

It is possible to calculate $\alpha(\omega)$ for particular gases, using perturbation theory, as shown in texts on quantum mechanics (such as *Quantum Mechanics* by P.C.W. Davies in this series).

These relations are true for dilute gases, where the atoms are so far apart as to be independent of one another. In dense gases, liquids and solids the polarising field on each atom is not the external field $\mathbf{E}$, but a local field $\mathbf{E}_{loc}$, which allows for the polarisation of neighbouring atoms. For dielectrics whose molecules do not have permanent dipole moments, that is non-polar dielectrics, a simple model is to assume that the local field is:

$$\mathbf{E}_{loc} = \mathbf{E} + \mathbf{E}_{out} + \mathbf{E}_{in}$$

where $\mathbf{E}_{out}$ is the field due to the polarisation of the dielectric outside a sphere of radius r_s, large compared with the intermolecular spacing a, surrounding the molecule, and $\mathbf{E}_{in}$ is the field due to the neighbouring molecules inside the sphere, as shown in Fig. 4.1(a). The polarised dielectric produces a surface charge density σ_p, which varies with the angle θ of a surface segment $dS = 2\pi.r_s \sin\theta.r_s \, d\theta$, such that:

$$\sigma_p dS = \mathbf{P}.\mathbf{dS} = -P\cos\theta \, dS \qquad [4.10]$$

where $\mathbf{dS}$ is in the direction of the outward normal to the charged surface. The field $\mathbf{E}_{out}$ is parallel to $\mathbf{E}$ and is therefore along the x axis in Fig. 4.1(b), so that:

$$\mathbf{E}_{out} = -(\sigma_p dS) \cos\theta / (4\pi\epsilon_0 r_s^2). \qquad [4.11]$$

Combining equations [4.10] and [4.11] and integrating over the surface of the sphere:

$$\mathbf{E}_{out} = \frac{\mathbf{P}}{2\epsilon_0} \int_0^\pi \cos^2\theta \sin\theta \, d\theta = \frac{\mathbf{P}}{3\epsilon_0}. \qquad [4.12]$$

The field $\mathbf{E}_{in}$ due to the neighbouring molecules is more difficult to determine. Lorentz showed that for molecules on a simple cubic lattice $\mathbf{E}_{in} = 0$. It is reasonable to suppose that a random array of molecules, as in a glass or a liquid, should similarly have $\mathbf{E}_{in} = 0$. Therefore in this model:

$$\mathbf{E}_{loc} = \mathbf{E} + \frac{\mathbf{P}}{3\epsilon_0}. \qquad [4.13]$$

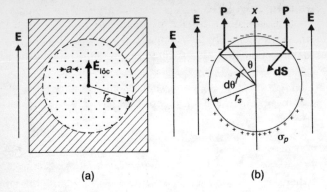

(a)   (b)

Fig. 4.1 (a) The local field E_{loc} in a dense dielectric on a molecule at 0 can be computed from the sum of the external field E, the field due to the polarised dielectric (shaded) E_{out} and the field E_{in} due to the neighbouring molecules inside a sphere of radius $r_s \gg a$, the intermolecular distance. (b) The field E_{out} is equivalent to that of a hollow sphere with a surface charge density σ_p due to the polarised dielectric

Similar arguments apply to the local electric field due to an electromagnetic wave, provided its wavelength $\lambda \gg a$, the intermolecular spacing. Therefore the dynamic polarisation of a dense dielectric differs from that of a gas (equation [4.9]) and becomes:

$$\mathbf{P} = N\alpha(\omega) \; \{\mathbf{E} + \mathbf{P}/(3\epsilon_0)\} \; . \qquad [4.14]$$

Solving this equation for α and using equation [4.1] we obtain

$$\left(\frac{N\alpha}{1 - \dfrac{N\alpha}{3\epsilon_0}} \right) = \frac{\mathbf{P}}{\mathbf{E}} = \epsilon_0 \chi_e = \epsilon_0 \, (\epsilon_r - 1)$$

which can be rearranged to give the *Clausius–Mossotti equation*:

$$\frac{N\alpha}{3\epsilon_0} = \left(\frac{\epsilon_r - 1}{\epsilon_r + 2} \right) . \qquad [4.15]$$

This equation approximates well to experiment for non-polar liquids and solids, showing that the local field model is valid over a wide range of densities. For example, for argon gas $\epsilon_r = 1.000545$ at NTP, but liquid argon at 87 K is 780 times as dense and has $\epsilon_r = 1.54$, compared with 1.50 that would be computed from equation [4.15].

In polar gases the effect of an applied electric field is to align the permanent dipole moments, $\mathbf{p_0}$, which otherwise are randomly orientated by the thermal motion of the molecules. The balance between the thermal agitation and the electrical alignment is similar to that for paramagnetics in a magnetic field and results in Curies' law for the polarisation:

$$\mathbf{P} = \left(\frac{Np_0^2}{3k_B T}\right) \mathbf{E}_{loc} \qquad [4.16]$$

where k_B is the Boltzmann constant and T the absolute temperature. Since the electronic polarisation of the Clausius–Mossotti model still takes place, the total polarisation will be the sum of equations [4.14] and [4.16]. Therefore for polar gases the Clausius–Mossotti equation [4.15] becomes:

$$\left(\frac{\epsilon_r - 1}{\epsilon_r + 2}\right) = \frac{N}{3\epsilon_0}\left(\alpha + \frac{p_0^2}{3k_B T}\right). \qquad [4.17]$$

Measurements of the permittivity as the function of temperature thus enable both the polarisability α and the dipole moment p_0 of the molecules in a polar dielectric to be obtained. However, unlike paramagnetics, polar molecules are not rotated in solid dielectrics by an electric field, since the intermolecular forces between the electric dipoles in a solid are too strong to be overcome by external fields. Even in a polar liquid the Lorentz approximation for the local field does not apply and so equation [4.17] is limited to polar gases.

4.2 Wave parameters in dielectrics

By dielectric media we mean gases, liquids or solids in which there are no free charges ($\rho_f = j_f = 0$) and in which magnetisation is negligible ($\mathbf{M} = 0$). Maxwell's equations in dielectric media are then:

$$\text{div } \mathbf{E} = - \text{ div } \mathbf{P}/\epsilon_0 \qquad [4.18]$$

$$\text{div } \mathbf{B} = 0 \qquad [4.19]$$

$$\text{curl } \mathbf{E} = -\frac{\partial \mathbf{B}}{\partial t} \qquad [4.20]$$

$$\text{curl } \mathbf{B} = \frac{1}{c^2}\,\frac{\partial}{\partial t}\left(\frac{\mathbf{P}}{\epsilon_0} + \mathbf{E}\right) \qquad [4.21]$$

Here equation [4.18] follows from equations [1.1], [1.11] and [1.13], equations [4.19] and [4.20] are unchanged from equations [1.2] and [1.3], while equation [4.21] is equation [1.4] combined with equation [1.22] and $\mu_0\epsilon_0 = c^{-2}$. In this form the equations are quite general and can be used for anisotropic and non-linear dielectrics. However, they are simplified for *isotropic* materials, in which there will be a uniform polarisation and so div $\mathbf{P} = -\rho_p = 0$, and for *linear* materials in which $\mathbf{P}$ will be proportional to $\mathbf{E}$ in amplitude, as well as being in the same direction as $\mathbf{E}$.

For such isotropic, linear dielectrics we can deduce a wave equation that is very similar to equation [3.3] for free space. As before, we have:

$$\text{curl curl } \mathbf{E} = -\frac{\partial}{\partial t}(\text{curl } \mathbf{B})$$

and

$$\text{curl curl } \mathbf{E} = \text{grad div } \mathbf{E} - \nabla^2 \mathbf{E} = -\nabla^2 \mathbf{E}.$$

Therefore:

$$\nabla^2 \mathbf{E} - \frac{1}{c^2}\,\frac{\partial}{\partial t^2}\left(\frac{\mathbf{P}}{\epsilon_0} + \mathbf{E}\right) = 0. \qquad [4.22]$$

Since, by equation [1.25], $\mathbf{D} = \epsilon_r\epsilon_0\mathbf{E}$ for linear, isotropic dielectrics and the electric displacement is defined by $\mathbf{D} = \epsilon_0\mathbf{E} + \mathbf{P}$ (equation [1.9]), a simple form of equation [4.22] is:

$$\nabla^2 \mathbf{E} = \frac{\epsilon_r}{c^2}\,\frac{\partial^2 E}{\partial t^2}\,. \qquad [4.23]$$

Following the solutions in section 3.2 of the similar wave equation in free space, we see that for a linearly-polarised plane wave

$$E_x = E_0\,\exp\,i\,(\omega t - kz) \qquad [4.24]$$

where now the phase velocity

$$v = \frac{\omega}{k} = \frac{c}{\sqrt{\epsilon_r}} \, . \qquad [4.25]$$

In physical optics we define the *refractive index*, n, of a medium as the ratio of the phase velocities of an electromagnetic wave in free space to that in the medium:

$$n = \frac{c}{v} = \sqrt{\epsilon_r} \, . \qquad [4.26]$$

We have already seen that the permittivity of a dielectric is frequency dependent and so the refractive index will also vary with frequency. In particular we can rewrite the Clausius-Mossotti equation ([4.15]) as:

$$\frac{n^2 - 1}{n^2 + 2} = \frac{N\alpha}{3\epsilon_0} \qquad [4.27]$$

and in this form it is often known as the *Lorentz–Lorenz equation* in studies of dielectric media at optical frequencies.

The magnetic vector of the electromagnetic wave in a dielectric bears a similar relation to the electric vector as that found for a plane wave in free space. Using Maxwell's third equation ([4.20]) it is easily seen that equation [3.18] becomes:

$$\mathbf{B} = \frac{1}{v} (\hat{\mathbf{k}} \times \mathbf{E}) \qquad [4.28]$$

where $\hat{\mathbf{k}}$ is a unit vector in the direction of propagation of the wave.

In dielectrics there can be losses, associated with the damping of the electronic oscillators in the non-polar model (equation [4.8]) where $\alpha(\omega)$ is complex. For electromagnetic waves this is seen as an attenuation of the wave as it penetrates a dielectric. The combined effects of frequency dependence and absorption at optical frequencies are represented by a *complex refractive index*:

$$n = n_R - i n_I \qquad [4.29]$$

where the real part $n_R = c/v$ is the ordinary index of equation

[4.26], while the imaginary part n_I corresponds to an attenuating wave. With this notation equation [4.24] for the wave becomes:

$$E_x = E_0 \ \exp \ i\omega \left(t - \frac{nz}{c} \right)$$

and

$$E_x = E_0 \ \exp \ i\omega \left(t - \frac{n_R z}{c} \right) \exp \left(- \frac{n_I \omega}{c} z \right) \ . \qquad [4.30]$$

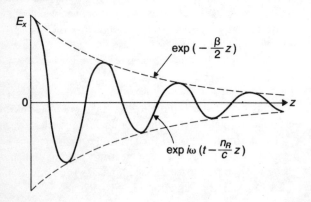

Fig. 4.2 The amplitude of an electromagnetic wave propagating along $0z$ at an instant of time has frequency $\omega/2\pi$, speed c/n_R and absorption coefficient $\beta/2$

The decaying amplitude of this wave is shown in Fig. 4.2, where β is the *absorption coefficient* derived from the intensity of the wave, proportional to E^2, decaying as $\exp(-\beta z)$, so that:

$$\beta = 2n_I \omega/c. \qquad [4.31]$$

At radio frequencies the use of a *complex permittivity*:

$$\epsilon_r = \epsilon_R - i\epsilon_I \qquad [4.32]$$

is common and dielectric loss is often expressed by the *loss tangent*, $\tan \delta = \epsilon_I/\epsilon_R$, as seen on an Argand diagram (Fig.4.3).

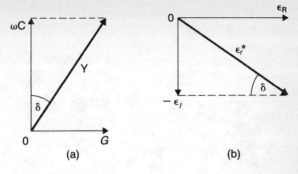

Fig. 4.3 A lossy dielectric has (a) an admittance $Y = G + i\omega C$, which is equivalent to (b) a complex permittivity $\epsilon_r = \epsilon_R - i\epsilon_I$, where the loss tangent, $\tan \delta = G/\omega C = \epsilon_I/\epsilon_R$

Here a lossy dielectric is said to have an admittance $Y = G + i\omega C$, where G is its conductance and ωC its susceptance, so that $\tan \delta = G/\omega C$.

4.3 Absorption and dispersion

The behaviour of dielectrics over the electromagnetic spectrum varies enormously. A familiar contrast is the different result obtained for a non-polar gas like air and a polar liquid like water. For air we find the permittivity is approximately constant from measurements in a radio-frequency bridge to that deduced from the refractive index optically using the relation $n^2 = \epsilon_r$ of equation [4.26], as shown in Table 4.1. On the other hand the permittivity of water at radio frequencies is far greater than that deduced from the refractive index. Most dielectrics exhibit resonances or relaxation peaks over the electromagnetic spectrum and we shall see how these can arise.

For non-polar gases at low pressures, we start with the Lorentz–Lorenz equation [4.27], where α is given by equation [4.8], i.e.

$$\frac{n^2 - 1}{n^2 + 2} = \frac{Ne^2}{3m\epsilon_0} \left(\frac{1}{\omega_0{}^2 - \omega^2 + i\gamma\omega} \right). \qquad [4.33]$$

Table 4.1 *Permittivities of common substances*

Frequency (Hz)	10^6	5×10^{14}
Air	$(\epsilon_r - 1) = 567 \times 10^{-6}$	576×10^{-6}
Water	$\epsilon_r = 80$	1.77

The Lorentz correction (equation [4.13]) for a local field can be neglected in dilute gases and if we assume any resonance produces only a weak absorption line ($\gamma \ll \omega_0$), then we can simplify equation [4.33]. Since by equation [4.26]

$$n^2 \cong n_R{}^2 = \epsilon_r$$

and from equations [4.1], [4.2] and [4.3]

$$\epsilon_r - 1 = \frac{\mathbf{P}}{\epsilon_0 \mathbf{E}} = \frac{N\alpha}{\epsilon_0} ,$$

equation [4.33] becomes

$$n_R{}^2 = 1 + \frac{Ne^2}{m\epsilon_0} \left\{ \frac{\omega_0{}^2 - \omega^2}{(\omega_0{}^2 - \omega^2)^2 + \gamma^2 \omega^2} \right\}. \qquad [4.34]$$

For a narrow absorption line (Fig. 4.4) the *natural width* is taken at the half-power points to be $2\Delta\omega$ and we can put

$$\omega_0{}^2 - \omega^2 = (\omega_0 + \omega)(\omega_0 - \omega) \cong 2\omega(\omega_0 - \omega)$$

and rewrite equation [4.34] as

$$n_R{}^2 = 1 + \frac{Ne^2}{2m\omega\epsilon_0} \left\{ \frac{(\omega_0 - \omega)}{(\omega_0 - \omega)^2 + (\Delta\omega)^2} \right\} \qquad [4.35]$$

since $\gamma\omega = (\omega_0{}^2 - \omega^2) = 2\omega\Delta\omega$ at the half-power points. Similarly for n_I we have $n_I \ll n_R$, $n_R \cong 1$, so that

$$\epsilon_I = 2n_R n_I \cong 2n_I$$

and therefore

$$n_I = \frac{Ne^2}{4m\omega\epsilon_0} \left\{ \frac{\Delta\omega}{(\omega_0 - \omega)^2 + (\Delta\omega)^2} \right\} . \qquad [4.36]$$

The real and imaginary parts of the complex refractive index near a narrow absorption line are shown in Fig. 4.4, where the real part exhibits the characteristic dispersion shape and the imaginary part shows a Lorentzian shape. In optics the line width is the total width $(2\Delta\omega)$ at the half-power points, whereas microwave spectroscopists commonly speak of the 'half-width' of the line $(\Delta\omega)$ at the half-power points.

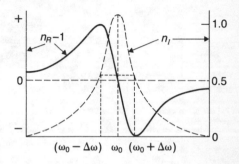

Fig. 4.4 The real n_R and imaginary n_I parts of the complex refractive index n near a narrow absorption line. The real part shows the characteristic dispersion shape at a resonance, while the imaginary part exhibits a Lorentzian shape

The behaviour of the refractive index n_R of a typical molecular gas over much of the electromagnetic spectrum is illustrated in Fig. 4.5. At very low frequencies, or long wavelengths, we are measuring n_R in the range $\omega \ll \omega_0$, where ω_0 is any resonant frequency of absorption in the molecule. This is the region where n_R is a maximum. At shorter wavelengths it passes through a succession of resonances, each of which has an absorption peak in n_I (Fig. 4.4). When the range of wavelengths does not include an absorption peak, n_R increases as λ decreases and this is known as *normal dispersion*. On the other hand, in the absorption regions n_R decreases as λ decreases, and such regions are said to exhibit *anomalous dispersion*. At the longer wavelengths the absorption peaks are associated with internal motions of the atoms in the molecules, such as rotations and vibrations, while at the shorter wavelengths the absorption is due to electronic transitions within the atoms. A full explanation of these absorption processes requires quantum mechanics, but a knowledge of elementary atomic physics is sufficient to understand that electronic transitions at optical wavelengths will be those of the outer shell, or valence, electrons, while the innermost shell, or core, electrons will produce resonant absorption at X-ray wavelengths.

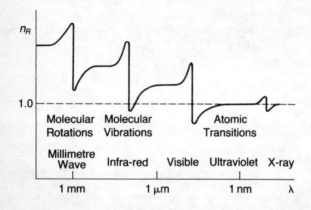

Fig. 4.5 • The refractive index of a molecular gas exhibits a variety of resonances over a wide spectrum and these are associated with molecular and atomic transitions. The resonances shown are not to scale, but illustrate the spectral regions for each type of resonance

At the high-frequency limit, $\omega \gg \omega_0$, all the Z electrons in an atom can be regarded as free, so that equation [4.32] becomes:

$$n_R{}^2 = 1 - \frac{ZNe^2}{m\epsilon_0\omega^2}$$

and, since $n_R \cong 1$,

$$n_R = 1 - ZNe^2/2m\,\epsilon_0\omega^2. \qquad [4.37]$$

Thus the refractive index is very close to, but slightly less than, unity for X-rays and γ-rays, and this is still true for dense media, such as metals, as we shall see in Chapter 6.

A different absorption process occurs in polar liquids, such as water, which show dielectric relaxation. When an electrostatic field is applied to a polar liquid the Brownian motion of the molecules acts to prevent the free rotation of the molecular dipoles and so dominates their motion. Removal of the electrostatic field then results in this polarization decaying with a *relaxation time*, τ, which is characteristic of the Brownian motion at a particular temperature T. The Lorentz correction for the local field in polar gases (equation [4.13]) does not apply to polar liquids, since normal electric fields produce only a small polarisation of the thermally agitated molecules. We therefore have, from equations [4.2], [4.3] and [4.16], that

$$\frac{\mathbf{P}}{\mathbf{E}} = N \left(\alpha + \frac{p_0^2}{3k_B T} \right) . \qquad [4.38]$$

Here the first term represents the instantaneously induced electronic polarization ($\mathbf{P}_i$) and the second is the time-dependent rotational polarization ($\mathbf{P}_r$) of the molecular dipoles. Thus

$$\mathbf{P} = \mathbf{P}_i + \mathbf{P}_r \qquad [4.39]$$

where the latter increases exponentially to a saturation value $\mathbf{P}_\infty$ that depends on the applied field:

$$\mathbf{P}_r = \mathbf{P}_\infty \left[1 - \exp\left(-t/\tau \right) \right] .$$

The rate of increase of the rotational polarization is

$$\frac{d\mathbf{P}_r}{dt} = \frac{\mathbf{P}_\infty \exp\left(-t/\tau \right)}{\tau} = \frac{\mathbf{P}_\infty - \mathbf{P}_r}{\tau} \qquad [4.40]$$

or

$$\mathbf{P}_\infty = \mathbf{P}_r + \frac{\tau d\mathbf{P}_r}{dt} = \left(\frac{N p_0^2}{3k_B T} \right) \mathbf{E}. \qquad [4.41]$$

When a radio-frequency field $E_0 \exp\left(i\omega t \right)$ is applied the rotational polarisation is

$$\mathbf{P}_r \left(t \right) = \mathbf{P}_r \left(0 \right) \exp\left(i\omega t \right)$$

so that equation [4.41] becomes

$$\mathbf{P}_r(t)(1 + i\omega\tau) = \left(\frac{Np_0{}^2}{3k_BT}\right)\mathbf{E}_0 \exp\,(i\omega t). \qquad [4.42]$$

Over a range of radio frequencies the permittivity relaxes (Fig. 4.6) from its static value, ϵ_s, to its high frequency value, ϵ_∞. From equation [4.39]

$$\mathbf{P} = \epsilon_0\,(\epsilon_s - 1)\,\mathbf{E}$$

and

$$\mathbf{P}_i = \epsilon_0\,(\epsilon_\infty - 1)\,\mathbf{E} \qquad [4.43]$$

so that

$$\mathbf{P}_\infty = \epsilon_0\,(\epsilon_s - \epsilon_\infty)\,\mathbf{E} = \left(\frac{Np_0{}^2}{3k_BT}\right)\mathbf{E}. \qquad [4.44]$$

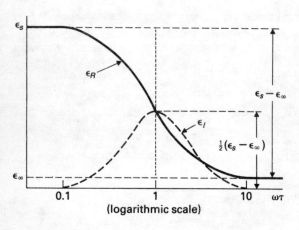

Fig. 4.6 The real ϵ_R and imaginary ϵ_I parts of the complex permittivity ϵ showing a broad Debye relaxation over a wide frequency range

In the presence of a high-frequency field the permittivity is complex and:

$$\mathbf{P}(t) = \epsilon_0\,(\epsilon_r - 1)\,\mathbf{E}(t). \qquad [4.45]$$

Combining the last four equations, we find

$$\epsilon_r = \epsilon_\infty + \frac{\epsilon_s - \epsilon_\infty}{1 + i\omega\tau}$$

or, using equation [4.32],

$$\epsilon_R = \epsilon_\infty + \left(\frac{\epsilon_s - \epsilon_\infty}{1 + \omega^2\tau^2}\right) \qquad [4.46]$$

$$\epsilon_I = \frac{(\epsilon_s - \epsilon_\infty)\,\omega\tau}{(1 + \omega^2\tau^2)} \; . \qquad [4.47]$$

These are the *Debye equations* and are plotted in Fig. 4.6 with the parameter $\omega\tau$ on a logarithmic scale. Measurements over a range of microwave frequencies were necessary for water, where $\epsilon_s = 80$ and $\tau = 10$ ps. However, the relaxation peak did not bring the value of ϵ_∞ down to $n_R{}^2$ measured optically, showing that absorption peaks of the type plotted in Fig. 4.5 occur in the infrared spectrum of water. It should be noted that a relaxation peak is very broad in frequency and that its height (ϵ_I) is less than half the fall in the permittivity, ϵ_R.

Chapter 5
Reflection and refraction

When electromagnetic waves are incident on the interface between two dielectrics the familiar phenomena of reflection and refraction take place. In this chapter we show that the wave properties of electromagnetic waves lead to the laws of reflection and refraction at plane surfaces, while their electromagnetic properties with the boundary conditions for electric and magnetic fields at dielectric interfaces lead to Fresnel's equations for plane-polarised waves. We conclude with a discussion of the special properties associated with waves incident at the Brewster angle and at angles greater than the critical angle.

5.1 Boundary relations

In elementary texts Gauss's laws for the fluxes of $\mathbf{D}$ and $\mathbf{B}$ and the circulation laws for $\mathbf{E}$ and $\mathbf{H}$ are used to show that at a boundary between two media of permittivities ϵ_1, ϵ_2 and permeabilities μ_1, μ_2 the normal components of $\mathbf{D}$ and $\mathbf{B}$ together with the tangential components of $\mathbf{E}$ and $\mathbf{H}$, are continuous. Following Feynman these boundary relations will be deduced by applying Maxwell's equations to a plane interface where there is a sharp discontinuity in material properties, that is ϵ and μ change within a fraction of a wavelength of an electromagnetic wave.

For a polarisable, magnetisable medium with *no free charges* we have, from the alternative form of Maxwell's equations (equations [1.14], [1.2], [1.3] and [1.23]):

$$\text{div } \mathbf{D} = 0 \qquad\qquad [5.1]$$

$$\text{div } \mathbf{B} = 0 \qquad\qquad [5.2]$$

$$\text{curl } \mathbf{E} = - \partial \mathbf{B}/\partial t \qquad\qquad [5.3]$$

$$\text{curl } \mathbf{H} = \partial \mathbf{D}/\partial t. \qquad\qquad [5.4]$$

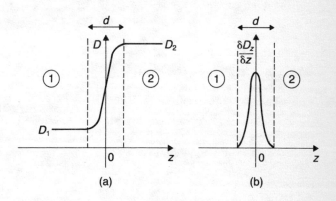

Fig. 5.1 (a) The electric displacement D at the interface of width d between two dielectrics 1, 2 is postulated to change from D_1 to D_2. (b) In consequence the z-component of div $\mathbf{D}$ peaks at the boundary

We assume that the plane interface between the two media is the xy plane, so that (Fig. 5.1) the z axis is normal to the interface. The physical properties at the boundary change over a distance $d \ll \lambda$, the wavelength of the electromagnetic wave that is to travel from medium 1 into medium 2. In Fig. 5.1(a) we have shown the electric displacement changing from D_1 to D_2 across the interface, but similar relations could exist for B, E and H.

At the boundary the three spatial coefficients of the components of these electromagnetic vectors behave very differently. The $\partial/\partial x$ and $\partial/\partial y$ coefficients of the field components will not change abruptly, while the $\partial/\partial z$ coefficients could peak sharply (Fig. 5.1(b)) if one of the field components changed rapidly during the narrow interface of width 'd'. So in applying Maxwell's equations we will consider the $\partial/\partial z$ coefficients only, as they dominate the interface.

From equations [5.1], we have

$$\frac{\partial D_x}{\partial x} + \frac{\partial D_y}{\partial y} + \frac{\partial D_z}{\partial z} = 0$$

so that, since $\partial D_x/\partial x = \partial D_y/\partial y = 0$, then $\partial D_z/\partial z$ must be zero at the interface and there can be no peak like Fig. 5.1(b). Therefore

$$D_{1z} = D_{2z}. \tag{5.5}$$

Similarly, from equation [5.2]

$$B_{1z} = B_{2z}. \tag{5.6}$$

On the other hand, equations [5.3] and [5.4] are vector equations where each vector component must be equal, giving for equation [5.3]:

$$\frac{\partial E_z}{\partial y} - \frac{\partial E_y}{\partial z} = -\frac{\partial B_x}{\partial t}$$

$$\frac{\partial E_x}{\partial z} - \frac{\partial E_z}{\partial x} = -\frac{\partial B_y}{\partial t}$$

$$\frac{\partial E_y}{\partial x} - \frac{\partial E_x}{\partial y} = -\frac{\partial B_z}{\partial t}.$$

In these equations only the components $\partial E_y/\partial z$ and $\partial E_x/\partial z$ could peak sharply at the interface, but the time derivatives of B will not have sharp peaks. Therefore E_y and E_x must be continuous at the interface and:

$$E_{1y} = E_{2y} \tag{5.7}$$

$$E_{1x} = E_{2x}. \tag{5.8}$$

Similarly, from equation [5.4]

$$H_{1y} = H_{2y} \tag{5.9}$$

$$H_{1x} = H_{2x}. \tag{5.10}$$

Equations [5.5] to [5.10] show which components of **D**, **B**, **E** and **H** are continuous across an interface and correspond exactly with the equations in elementary texts, where the normal components of **D** and **B** and the tangential components of **E** and **H** are continuous at a boundary. We shall apply these boundary conditions to the electromagnetic fields of a plane wave to determine the Fresnel equations, but first we consider the relationship of the wave properties of an electromagnetic wave across an interface (Fig. 5.2).

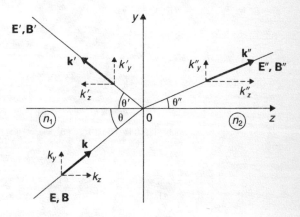

Fig. 5.2 An electromagnetic wave incident at an angle θ in the yz plane to an interface in the xy plane separating two dielectric media of refractive indices n_1 and n_2 produces a reflected wave at angle θ' and a transmitted wave at angle θ''

It is easily shown from Maxwell's equations (equations [5.1] to [5.4]) that the wave equations for an electromagnetic wave in a polarisable, magnetisable medium are (see Chapter 4, exercise 2):

$$\nabla^2 \mathbf{E} = \frac{1}{v^2} \frac{\partial^2 \mathbf{E}}{\partial t^2} \qquad [5.11]$$

$$\nabla^2 \mathbf{B} = \frac{1}{v^2} \frac{\partial^2 \mathbf{B}}{\partial t^2} \qquad [5.12]$$

where $v^2 = c^2/(\mu_r \epsilon_r) = c^2/n^2$. For a plane wave of wave vector **k** and frequency ω in such a medium, we have, by comparison with equations [4.24] and [4.28], therefore:

$$\mathbf{E} = \mathbf{E}_0 \, \exp \, i\,(\omega t - \mathbf{k.r})$$

$$\mathbf{B} = \frac{\hat{\mathbf{k}} \times \mathbf{E}}{v} = \frac{\mathbf{k} \times \mathbf{E}}{\omega} \tag{5.13}$$

where $\mathbf{E}$, $\mathbf{B}$ are the electric and magnetic vectors of the plane wave at a point $\mathbf{r}$ from the origin at time t. Following its interaction with the xy plane of the surface (Fig. 5.2) the reflected wave is:

$$\mathbf{E}' = \mathbf{E}_0' \, \exp \, i\,(\omega't - \mathbf{k'.r})$$

$$\mathbf{B}' = (\mathbf{k}' \times \mathbf{E}')/\omega' \tag{5.14}$$

and the transmitted wave is:

$$\mathbf{E}'' = \mathbf{E}_0'' \, \exp \, i\,(\omega'' t - \mathbf{k''.r}) \tag{5.15}$$

$$\mathbf{B}'' = (\mathbf{k}'' \times \mathbf{E}'')/\omega''.$$

If we choose axes such that the incident wave vector $\mathbf{k}$ is in the yz plane, then

$$\mathbf{k.r} = k_y y + k_z z. \tag{5.16}$$

At the interface ($z = 0$) the sum of the incident and reflected electric fields must equal that transmitted, so that

$$\mathbf{E}_0 \, \exp \, i\,(\omega t - k_y y) + \mathbf{E}_0' \, \exp \, i\,(\omega't - k_y' y)$$

$$= \mathbf{E}_0'' \, \exp \, i\,(\omega''t - k_y'' y). \tag{5.17}$$

For this to be true at all times t and for all points $(y, 0)$ on the interface, clearly

$$\omega = \omega' = \omega'' \tag{5.18}$$

so that there can be no change of frequency occurring. Since the speed v_1 of the incident and reflected waves must be the same

$$\mathbf{k.k} = k^2 = \frac{\omega^2}{v_1{}^2} = k'^2, \tag{5.19}$$

and

$$k''^2 = \frac{v_1{}^2 k^2}{v_2{}^2} = \frac{n_2{}^2 k^2}{n_1{}^2}. \tag{5.20}$$

But for equation [5.17] to be true for all y

$$k_y = k_y' = k_y''. \tag{5.21}$$

To satisfy both [5.19] and [5.21] the reflected wave must have $k_z' = -k_z$ and so (Fig. 5.2) the angle of incidence θ equals the angle of reflection θ' and is in the yz plane. Electromagnetic waves therefore obey the *laws of reflection*.

For the transmitted wave, equations [5.20] and [5.21] give:

$$k_z''^2 = \left(\frac{n_2^2}{n_1^2}\right) k^2 - k_y^2 \tag{5.22}$$

which is true for all dielectrics, including the conditions under which n is complex (equation [4.29]). When n_1 and n_2 are real, that is away from resonances (Fig. 4.5), then

$$k_y = k \sin \theta = k_y'' = k'' \sin \theta''$$

or

$$\frac{\sin \theta''}{\sin \theta} = \frac{k}{k''} = \frac{n_1}{n_2} \tag{5.23}$$

which is the *law of refraction* discovered by Snell experimentally in 1621.

5.2   Fresnel's equations

Although we have proved that electromagnetic waves obey the experimental laws of reflection and refraction at plane dielectric interfaces, these laws follow from any wave theory having the general wave equation [3.5]. The distinctive features of electromagnetism are found in the amplitudes of the reflected and transmitted waves that fulfil the electromagnetic boundary conditions (equations [5.5] to [5.10]). In general, as we saw in section 3.2, a plane electromagnetic wave is elliptically polarised, but any electric polarisation can always be represented as the sum of an electric vector normal to the plane of incidence (Fig. 5.3(a)) and one parallel to it (Fig. 5.3(b)). The magnetic vectors then follow from the relations $\mathbf{B} = (\mathbf{k} \times \mathbf{E})/\omega$ for each wave.

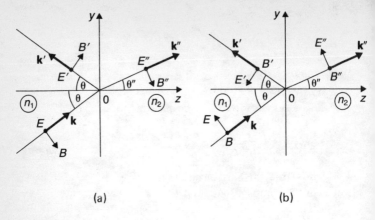

(a)   (b)

Fig. 5.3 (a) A plane-polarised electromagnetic wave with the electric vectors *normal* to the plane of incidence and directed out of the figure is partially reflected and transmitted. (b) A plane-polarised electromagnetic wave with the electric vectors *parallel* to the plane of incidence is partially reflected and transmitted. The magnetic vectors are directed out of the figure

E normal or TE polarisation

In Fig. 5.3(a) the incident electric vector is normal to the yz plane in the $-x$ direction (out of the figure), so that the incident magnetic vector is in the yz plane (compare Fig. 3.3). For isotropic dielectrics the induced oscillations will be parallel to the incident ones, so that E', B' and E'', B'' are as shown. At the interface ($z = 0$), the superposition of the electric fields, equation [5.17], with equations [5.18] and [5.21] becomes:

$$E_0 + E_0' = E_0''. \qquad [5.24]$$

For the magnetic vectors in the yz plane only their y components, equation [5.9], provide any additional information. Since $\mathbf{B} = \mu_r\mu_0\mathbf{H} = (\mathbf{k} \times \mathbf{E})/\omega$, equation [5.9] becomes:

$$\frac{(\mathbf{k} \times \mathbf{E})_{1y}}{\mu_{r1}\mu_0\omega} = \frac{(\mathbf{k} \times \mathbf{E})_{2y}}{\mu_{r2}\mu_0\omega}$$

which simplifies to:

$$\frac{(\hat{\mathbf{k}} \times \mathbf{E})_{1y}}{Z_1} = \frac{(\hat{\mathbf{k}} \times \mathbf{E})_{2y}}{Z_2} \qquad [5.25]$$

since $k = \omega/v$ and where, from equation [3.38], the wave impedance is given by:

$$Z = \frac{E_x}{H_y} = \mu_r \mu_0 v. \qquad [5.26]$$

Hence, in terms of the wave impedances of each medium:

$$\frac{E_0 \cos \theta}{Z_1} - \frac{E_0' \cos \theta}{Z_1} = \frac{E_0'' \cos \theta''}{Z_2}. \qquad [5.27]$$

Combining equations [5.24] and [5.27], the reflected and transmitted amplitudes for $\mathbf{E}$ normal to the plane of incidence or TE
polarisation are

$$\left(\frac{E_0'}{E_0}\right)_{\text{TE}} = \frac{Z_2 \cos \theta - Z_1 \cos \theta''}{Z_2 \cos \theta + Z_1 \cos \theta''} \qquad [5.28]$$

and

$$\left(\frac{E_0''}{E_0}\right)_{\text{TE}} = \frac{2Z_2 \cos \theta}{Z_2 \cos \theta + Z_1 \cos \theta''}. \qquad [5.29]$$

At optical frequencies $\mu_{r1} = \mu_{r2} = 1$, $n^2 = \epsilon_r$ and so $Z_1/Z_2 = v_1/v_2 = n_2/n_1 = \sin \theta/\sin \theta''$, by equation [5.23]. Hence these
amplitude equations simplify to:

$$\left(\frac{E_0'}{E_0}\right)_{\text{TE}} = \frac{\sin(\theta'' - \theta)}{\sin(\theta'' + \theta)}, \quad \left(\frac{E_0''}{E_0}\right)_{\text{TE}} = \frac{2 \sin \theta'' \cos \theta}{\sin(\theta'' + \theta)}. \qquad [5.30]$$

E parallel or TM polarisation

In Fig. 5.3(b) the incident magnetic vector is normal to the yz
plane in the $-x$ direction, so that the incident electric vector is
in the yz plane, as given by $\mathbf{B} = (\mathbf{k} \times \mathbf{E})/\omega$. The relevant boundary
equations are now [5.7] and [5.10], giving:

$$(E_0 - E_0') \cos \theta = E_0'' \cos \theta'' \qquad [5.31]$$

and

$$\frac{E_0}{Z_1} + \frac{E_0{}'}{Z_1} = \frac{E_0{}''}{Z_2} .$$ [5.32]

Solving equations [5.31] and [5.32] for the reflected and transmitted amplitudes for **E** parallel to plane of incidence or TM polarisation gives

$$\left(\frac{E_0{}'}{E}\right)_{\text{TM}} = \frac{Z_2 \cos\theta'' - Z_1 \cos\theta}{Z_2 \cos\theta'' + Z_1 \cos\theta}$$ [5.33]

and

$$\left(\frac{E_0{}''}{E_0}\right)_{\text{TM}} = \frac{2Z_2 \cos\theta}{Z_2 \cos\theta'' + Z_1 \cos\theta} .$$ [5.34]

At optical frequencies these simplify to:

$$\left(\frac{E_0{}'}{E_0}\right)_{\text{TM}} = \frac{\tan(\theta - \theta'')}{\tan(\theta + \theta'')},$$

$$\left(\frac{E_0{}''}{E_0}\right)_{\text{TM}} = \frac{2\cos\theta \sin\theta''}{\sin(\theta + \theta'') \cos(\theta - \theta'')} .$$ [5.35]

Equations [5.30] and [5.35], known as Fresnel's equations after their discoverer, apply at optical frequencies to transparent media, where the refractive indices are real. They are drawn for air to glass in Fig. 5.4.

Polarisation by reflection

For a particular angle of incidence, known as the Brewster angle, the reflected wave for TM polarisation has zero amplitude: the reflection disappears. The Brewster angle is, from equation [5.35], given by

$$(\theta_{\text{B}} + \theta'') = \pi/2$$

which, with Snell's law, becomes:

$$n_1 \sin\theta_{\text{B}} = n_2 \sin\left(\frac{\pi}{2} - \theta_{\text{B}}\right) = n_2 \cos\theta_{\text{B}}$$

or

$$\tan \theta_B = \frac{n_2}{n_1}. \tag{5.36}$$

At this angle an unpolarised wave would be reflected as a plane polarised wave with TE polarisation, the TM polarisation being fully transmitted. For air to glass, $n_2/n_1 = 1.5$ and the Brewster angle is $56°$.

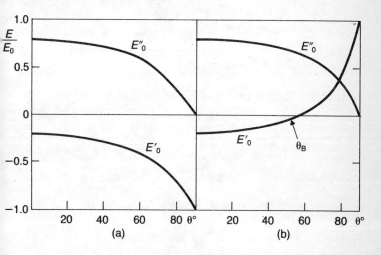

Fig. 5.4 The reflected (E_0') and transmitted (E_0'') relative amplitudes from Fresnel's equations: (a) transverse electric (TE) polarisation; (b) transverse magnetic (TM) polarisation, for an air/glass interface with $n_2/n_1 = 1.5$. The Brewster angle is θ_B

The phase of the reflected wave for TE polarisation (Fig. 5.4(a)) depends only on n_2/n_1 and is always negative for $n_2 > n_1$. On the other hand for TM polarisation the phase changes from negative to positive at the Brewster angle (Fig. 5.4(b)) so that its sign depends on the angle of incidence.

5.3 Energy flow at a boundary

In section 3.4 we showed that the equation of conservation of energy flow was:

$$-\frac{\partial u}{\partial t} = \text{div}\,\mathscr{S} + \mathbf{E}.\mathbf{j} \qquad [3.27]$$

where $\mathbf{j}$ was the current produced by a charge q moving at speed v, u was the energy density and $\mathscr{S}$ the flux of electromagnetic energy. In applying it to free space, we found that $\mathscr{S} = \mathbf{E} \times \mathbf{H}$, the Poynting vector. We will now show that it remains $\mathbf{E} \times \mathbf{H}$ in a medium.

The current $\mathbf{j}$ in a medium will be that due to the free charges j_f, given by equation [1.23], so that

$$\mathbf{E}.\mathbf{j} = \mathbf{E}.\text{curl}\,\mathbf{H} - \mathbf{E}.\frac{\partial \mathbf{D}}{\partial t}. \qquad [5.37]$$

Using the vector identity for div $(\mathbf{A} \times \mathbf{B})$ from Appendix 4

$$\mathbf{E}.\,\text{curl}\,\mathbf{H} = \text{div}\,(\mathbf{H} \times \mathbf{E}) + \mathbf{H}.\text{curl}\,\mathbf{E}$$

which, with Maxwell's equation for curl $\mathbf{E}$, becomes

$$\mathbf{E}.\text{curl}\,\mathbf{H} = \text{div}\,(\mathbf{H} \times \mathbf{E}) - \frac{\partial}{\partial t}\left(\frac{\mathbf{H}.\mathbf{B}}{2}\right).$$

Substituting this expression in equation [5.37] gives

$$\mathbf{E}.\mathbf{j} = \text{div}\,(\mathbf{H} \times \mathbf{E}) - \frac{\partial}{\partial t}\left\{\frac{\mathbf{E}.\mathbf{D}}{2} + \frac{\mathbf{H}.\mathbf{B}}{2}\right\}. \qquad [5.38]$$

Comparing equations [5.38] and [3.27], we see that for energy flow and energy density in a medium:

$$\mathscr{S} = \mathbf{E} \times \mathbf{H} \qquad [5.39]$$

$$u = \frac{1}{2}\,\{\mathbf{E}.\mathbf{D} + \mathbf{H}.\mathbf{B}\} \qquad [5.40]$$

where for linear, isotropic media, $\mathbf{B} = \mu_r \mu_0 \mathbf{H}$ and $\mathbf{D} = \epsilon_r \epsilon_0 \mathbf{E}$. Although the Poynting vector has not changed, the energy density now includes the energy associated with the polarisation current density $\partial \mathbf{P}/\partial t$ and the magnetic current density curl $\mathbf{M}$ (equation [1.22]) which were shown in Chapter 1 to lead to Maxwell equation [1.23]. That is why equation [5.40] for energy density in a medium differs from equation [3.32] for energy density in free space.

At optical frequencies in dielectrics we have n real, so that the **E** and **H** vectors in an electromagnetic wave are in phase and the electric and magnetic energy densities are equal:

$$\frac{1}{2}\epsilon_r\epsilon_0 E^2 = \frac{1}{2}\mu_r\mu_0 H^2 . \qquad [5.41]$$

The total energy density is therefore $\epsilon_r\epsilon_0 E^2 = n^2\epsilon_0 E^2$ and the average energy density $\langle u \rangle = n^2\epsilon_0 E^2_{\text{rms}}$. Therefore the average Poynting vector

$$\langle \mathscr{S} \rangle = \frac{1}{2}E_0 H_0 \hat{\mathbf{k}} \qquad [5.42]$$

so that the intensity

$$\langle \mathscr{S} \rangle = \frac{1}{2}\left(\frac{\epsilon_r\epsilon_0}{\mu_r\mu_0}\right)^{\frac{1}{2}}E_0{}^2 = \frac{E_0{}^2}{2Z} \qquad [5.43]$$

or

$$\langle \mathscr{S} \rangle = \frac{1}{2}v(\epsilon_r\epsilon_0)E_0{}^2 = v\langle u \rangle \qquad [5.44]$$

as would be expected for the average energy flow across unit area.

The *reflection coefficient* or *reflectance R* is the ratio of the average energy flux per second reflected to that incident on an interface, so that, from equations [5.42] and [5.43]

$$R = \frac{\langle \mathscr{S}' \rangle.\hat{\mathbf{n}}}{\langle \mathscr{S} \rangle.\hat{\mathbf{n}}} = \frac{E_0{}'^2}{E_0{}^2} \qquad [5.45]$$

where $\hat{\mathbf{n}}$ is a unit vector normal to the interface. Similarly the *transmission coefficient* or *transmittance T* is:

$$T = \frac{\langle \mathscr{S}'' \rangle.\hat{\mathbf{n}}}{\langle \mathscr{S} \rangle.\hat{\mathbf{n}}} = \frac{Z_1 E_0{}''^2 \cos\theta''}{Z_2 E_0{}^2 \cos\theta} . \qquad [5.46]$$

When energy is conserved at the interface, we always have:

$$R + T = 1. \qquad [5.47]$$

Using Fresnel's equations for $E_0{}'$, $E_0{}''$, we find for TE polarisation

$$R_{\text{TE}} = \left(\frac{Z_2 \cos \theta - Z_1 \cos \theta''}{Z_2 \cos \theta + Z_1 \cos \theta''} \right)^2 = \frac{\sin^2 (\theta'' - \theta)}{\sin^2 (\theta'' + \theta)} \quad [5.48]$$

and for TM polarisation

$$R_{\text{TM}} = \left(\frac{Z_2 \cos \theta'' - Z_1 \cos \theta}{Z_2 \cos \theta'' + Z_1 \cos \theta} \right)^2 = \frac{\tan^2 (\theta - \theta'')}{\tan^2 (\theta + \theta'')} \quad [5.49]$$

where the second expressions apply at optical frequencies where $Z_1/Z_2 = n_2/n_1 = \sin \theta / \sin \theta''$. In both cases the transmittances can be found using equation [5.47] or from equations [5.46], [5.29] and [5.34]. The reflectances for air/glass with $n_2/n_1 = 1.5$ are shown in Fig. 5.5. At the Brewster angle $R_{\text{TM}} = 0$, as expected.

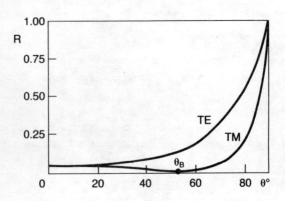

Fig. 5.5 The reflectances for an air/glass interface when transverse electric (TE) and transverse magnetic (TM) radiation is incident at angle θ. The Brewster angle is θ_B

At normal incidence ($\theta = 0$), both equations [5.48] and [5.49] give

$$R_0 = \left(\frac{Z_2 - Z_1}{Z_2 + Z_1} \right)^2 = \left(\frac{n_1 - n_2}{n_1 + n_2} \right)^2 \quad [5.50]$$

so that:

$$T_0 = \left(\frac{2Z_2}{Z_2 + Z_1}\right)^2 = \left(\frac{2n_1}{n_1 + n_2}\right)^2. \qquad [5.51]$$

5.4 Total internal reflection

When radiation is being transmitted from a dense to a less dense medium, for example glass to air, with $n_1 > n_2$, then Snell's law (equation [5.23]) gives

$$\sin \theta'' = \frac{n_1}{n_2} \sin \theta.$$

There will therefore be a critical angle of incidence θ_c for which θ'' has its maximum value of $90°$

$$\sin \theta_c = \frac{n_2}{n_1}. \qquad [5.52]$$

For incidence at all angles $\theta > \theta_c$, there can only be 'total internal reflection'.

This phenomenon can be understood if we go back to equation [5.22], which applies when n is complex:

$$k_z''^2 = \left(\frac{n_2}{n_1}\right)^2 k^2 - k_y^2.$$

Since $k^2 = \omega^2/v_1^2$, $k_y = k \sin \theta$, and $v_1^2/v_2^2 = n_2^2/n_1^2$

$$k_z''^2 = \frac{\omega^2}{v_2^2} \left(1 - \frac{n_1^2}{n_2^2} \sin^2 \theta\right). \qquad [5.53]$$

Now when $\theta > \theta_c$, $n_1\sin \theta/n_2 > 1$ and so k_z'' is an imaginary number, say $- ik_I$, showing that the amplitude is decaying in a similar way to imaginary parts of n and ϵ_r in equations [4.29] and [4.32]. Hence the transmitted wave, equation [5.15], becomes

$$E'' = E_0'' \exp(-k_I z) \exp i(\omega t - k_y y) \qquad [5.54]$$

and we see that it travels only a short distance into the second medium, decaying in amplitude by $1/e$ within $\lambda/2\pi$. The existence of this evanescent wave can be demonstrated most conveniently with microwaves (say $\lambda = 3$ cm), as illustrated in Fig. 5.6, where

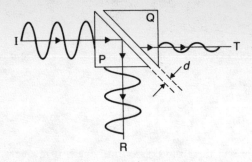

Fig. 5.6 An incident microwave beam I is internally reflected by the prism P to the receiver R, but a small transmitted signal can be observed at T when a second prism Q is at a distance $d < \lambda$, the microwave wavelength. This demonstrates that an evanescent wave accompanies total internal reflection

the internally reflected signal at R will decrease when the second prism Q is brought within a distance $d < \lambda$ and a transmitted signal can be detected at T.

Chapter 6
Electromagnetic waves in conductors

Electromagnetic waves propagate with their electric and magnetic fields oscillating about the direction of propagation (Fig. 3.6) so that when they interact with matter the largest effects come from the lightest charged particles, the electrons. In dielectrics the electrons are bound charges and in Chapter 4 we found that the polarisation was characterised by the atomic polarisability $\alpha(\omega)$, given by the Clausius–Mossotti and Lorentz–Lorenz equations.

Table 6.1 *Density of charge carriers in conductors*

Conductor	Example	Density, N (m^{-3})
Noble metal	Copper, silver, gold	6×10^{28}–9×10^{28}
Alkali metal	Sodium, caesium	8×10^{27}–5×10^{28}
Semi-metal	Bismuth, antimony, arsenic	3×10^{23}–2×10^{26}
Semiconductor	Extrinsic germanium	5×10^{20}–10^{24}
Dense plasma	Solar, laser, discharge	10^{20}–10^{26}
Weak plasma	Ionosphere, space	10^{6}–10^{11}

In conductors these effects are still present, but they are normally very small compared with the interactions with the conduction electrons. The densities of these carriers (Table 6.1) varies from 9×10^{28} m^{-3} in a noble metal to about 10^{20}–10^{24} m^{-3} in semiconductors and dense plasmas, but can be as little as 10^{11} m^{-3} in weakly ionised plasmas like the ionosphere, while interstellar gas has a density of about 10^{6} m^{-3}. Besides the density, the most important parameters for the propagation of electromagnetic waves are the relaxation time τ between collisions of the carriers, which determines the conductivity, and the frequency $(\omega/2\pi)$ of the wave.

6.1 Wave parameters in conductors

Classically a conducting medium obeys Ohm's law:

$$\mathbf{j}_f = \sigma \mathbf{E} \tag{6.1}$$

where σ is the electrical conductivity (SI unit $= $ S m^{-1}) of the medium, and has net charge density $\rho = 0$. Hence Maxwell's equations in a conductor are:

$$\text{div } \mathbf{E} = 0 \tag{6.2}$$

$$\text{div } \mathbf{B} = 0 \tag{6.3}$$

$$\text{curl } \mathbf{E} = -\frac{\partial \mathbf{B}}{\partial t} \tag{6.4}$$

$$\text{curl}\left(\frac{\mathbf{B}}{\mu_r \mu_0}\right) = \sigma \mathbf{E} + \epsilon_r \epsilon_0 \frac{\partial \mathbf{E}}{\partial t} \tag{6.5}$$

where the first three equations follow from equations [1.1], [1.2] and [1.3]. The fourth equation, combining equations [1.23], [1.24], [1.25] and [6.1], is valid for linear, isotropic conductors. We follow the same procedure as in dielectrics, putting

$$\text{curl curl } \mathbf{E} = \text{grad div } \mathbf{E} - \nabla^2 \mathbf{E} = -\nabla^2 \mathbf{E}$$

and hence find:

$$\nabla^2 \mathbf{E} = \mu_r \mu_0 \, \sigma \frac{\partial \mathbf{E}}{\partial t} + \mu_r \mu_0 \, \epsilon_r \epsilon_0 \frac{\partial^2 \mathbf{E}}{\partial t^2} . \tag{6.6}$$

Similarly

$$\nabla^2 \mathbf{H} = \mu_r \mu_0 \, \sigma \frac{\partial \mathbf{H}}{\partial t} + \mu_r \mu_0 \, \epsilon_r \epsilon_0 \frac{\partial^2 \mathbf{H}}{\partial t^2} . \tag{6.7}$$

In both equations, on the right-hand side the first term is derived from the conduction current and the second term from the displacement current.

As before, a linearly-polarised plane wave travelling along the z axis could have as its electric vector

$$E_x = E_0 \exp i\,(\omega t - kz) \qquad [6.8]$$

where, from equation [6.6]

$$-k^2 = i\,\omega\mu_r\mu_0\sigma - \omega^2\mu_r\mu_0\epsilon_r\epsilon_0$$

or

$$k^2 = \frac{\omega^2}{c^2}\left(1 - \frac{i\sigma}{\omega\epsilon_r\epsilon_0}\right)\left(\mu_r\epsilon_r\right) . \qquad [6.9]$$

The wave number is therefore complex and can be written:

$$k = k_R - ik_I \qquad [6.10]$$

so that the equation of the wave, [6.8], becomes

$$E_x = E_0 \exp i\,(\omega t - k_R z) \exp\,(-k_I z). \qquad [6.11]$$

This is an oscillatory field with decaying amplitude, similar to that shown in Fig. 4.2. However, in a *good conductor* $\sigma/\omega\epsilon_r\epsilon_0 \gg 1$ for frequencies up to at least the microwave range and so equations [6.9] and [6.10] yield (with $c^{-2} = \mu_0\epsilon_0$) the simple result:

$$k = \left(\frac{\mu_r\mu_0\omega\sigma}{2}\right)^{1/2}(1-i). \qquad [6.12]$$

In this case the wave is heavily attenuated, falling to $1/e$ of its initial amplitude in a distance

$$\delta = \frac{1}{k_I} = \left(\frac{2}{\mu_r\mu_0\omega\sigma}\right)^{1/2}. \qquad [6.13]$$

The distance δ is called the *skin depth* and is much less than the wavelength, $2\pi k$ of the electromagnetic wave in the conductor, as shown in Fig. 6.1. (It should not be confused with the penetration depth, Λ, in a superconductor, which refers to the decay of a static magnetic field, the Meissner effect.)

The magnetic vector of the linearly-polarised plane wave can be found by substituting E_x from equation [6.8] in the third Maxwell equation [6.4] to give

$$\begin{vmatrix} \hat{\mathbf{i}} & \hat{\mathbf{j}} & \hat{\mathbf{k}} \\ 0 & 0 & -ik \\ E_x & 0 & 0 \end{vmatrix} = -i\omega\,(B_x\hat{\mathbf{i}} + B_y\hat{\mathbf{j}} + B_z\hat{\mathbf{k}}).$$

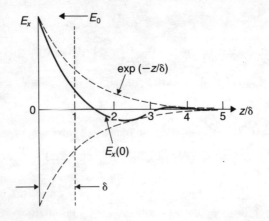

Fig. 6.1 An electromagnetic wave is heavily attenuated in a good conductor, penetrating less than a wavelength $(2\pi k)$, where δ is the skin depth given by equation [6.13]

Hence:

$$B_y = \frac{k}{\omega}\,E_x \quad \text{or} \quad H_y = \left(\frac{k}{\mu_r\mu_0\omega}\right)E_x \qquad [6.14]$$

where k is given by equation [6.12] in a good conductor. For this case we obtain:

$$\frac{E_x}{H_y} = \frac{\mu_r\mu_0\omega}{k} = \left(\frac{\mu_r\mu_0\omega}{\sigma}\right)^{1/2} \exp i\,(\pi/4) \qquad [6.15]$$

showing that E leads H by $45°$ in good conductors, in contrast to free space and dielectrics where E and H are in phase (Fig. 3.6). This difference arises from the dominance of the conduction current terms in equations [6.6] and [6.7] over the displacement current terms in good conductors. In terms of the skin depth the electric and magnetic vectors are therefore:

$$E_x = E_0 \exp i\,(\omega t - z/\delta)\exp(-z/\delta) \qquad [6.16]$$

$$H_y = \left(\frac{\sigma\delta E_0}{\sqrt{2}}\right)\exp i\,\left(\omega t - \frac{z}{\delta} - \frac{\pi}{4}\right)\exp\left(-\frac{z}{\delta}\right). \qquad [6.17]$$

The skin depth for a good conductor like copper is given by $\delta = (2/\mu_0\sigma\omega)^{1/2}$ and so becomes very small at microwave frequencies. For example, at 10 GHz in pure copper at 293 K, $\delta = 0.67\ \mu m$, falling to as little as 10 nm at 4 K, so that a thin plating of copper is all that is needed to absorb microwave radiation. At radio frequencies the resistance R_{rf} of a cylindrical wire is very different from its zero-frequency resistance R_0, since the r.f. fields only penetrate into a surface sheath of thickness about δ. Therefore the r.f. resistance is:

$$R_{rf} = \frac{l}{\sigma\,(2\pi r\delta)} = \frac{rR_0}{2\delta} \qquad [6.18]$$

and hence much finer wires can be used to provide low-resistance leads, often in the form of a braid, at radio frequencies, at much less cost than the rods necessary for direct currents.

.2   Wave impedance and reflectance

The wave impedance of a good conductor, from equations [5.26], [6.12] and [6.15], is:

$$Z = \frac{E_x}{H_y} = \frac{\mu_r\mu_0\omega}{k} = \left(\frac{2\mu_r\mu_0\omega}{\sigma}\right)^{1/2}\frac{1}{(1-i)}.$$

Substituting for δ from equation [6.13] this becomes

$$Z = \frac{(1+i)}{\sigma\delta} \qquad [6.19]$$

and has the value $0.025\,(1+i)\ \Omega$ for copper at 10 GHz. This small value of wave impedance shows that the electric field is much less than the magnetic field and so the electromagnetic energy in a good conductor is nearly all magnetic energy. Since the wave impedance is also much less than that for free space, $Z_0 = 377 \ \Omega$ (equation [3.40]), a microwave incident from air on to a metal is almost totally reflected.

The analysis of the reflected and transmitted waves formed when a plane wave is incident from a dielectric on to a conductor follows similar lines to those used for dielectrics in the previous chapter. Since the wave number and the wave impedance are complex for conductors, the phase changes at the boundary, which for dielectrics are always 0 or π, now vary, so that in general a plane-polarised wave after reflection will be elliptically polarised. The simplest case is that for normal incidence where, from equation [5.50], the reflectance is:

$$R_0 = \left(\frac{Z_2 - Z_1}{Z_2 + Z_1} \right)^2$$

and, for an air to metal reflection, $Z_1 = \mu_0 c$ and $Z_2 = (1 + i)/\sigma \delta$. Hence:

$$R_0 = \left| \frac{(1 + i) - \mu_0 c \sigma \delta}{(1 + i) + \mu_0 c \sigma \delta} \right|^2$$

which can be simplified if we put $a = \mu_0 c \sigma \delta$, to give

$$R_0 = \left| \frac{(1 - a) + i}{(1 + a) + i} \right|^2 = \frac{2 - 2a + a^2}{2 + 2a + a^2} .$$

For copper at 293 K, $a = 4\pi \times 10^{-7} \times 3 \times 10^8 \times 6 \times 10^7 \delta = 2.3 \times 10^{10} \delta$, so that at microwave frequencies $a \gg 1$. Hence:

$$R_0 = \frac{1 - \dfrac{2}{a} + \dfrac{2}{a^2}}{1 + \dfrac{2}{a} + \dfrac{2}{a^2}} \cong 1 - \frac{4}{a}$$

giving

$$R_0 = 1 - \frac{4}{\mu_0 c \sigma \delta} \qquad\qquad [6.20]$$

as the reflectance at normal incidence of microwave radiation on a good conductor.

The almost perfect reflectance of metals for electromagnetic radiation in classical theory is associated with their high absorption with a few skin depths (Fig. 6.1). This is an example of the general rule for radiation, that 'good absorbers are good reflectors' at a particular frequency, and comes from the large value of the imaginary $k_I = 1/\delta$. Dried red ink can sometimes be seen to give a greenish metallic reflection, showing that it absorbs green light, reflects green and transmits red.

The real part of the wave number, k_R, from equation [6.12], is also large and so the phase velocity v of a radio wave or microwave in a metal is very small, since:

$$v = \frac{\omega}{k_R} = \left(\frac{2\omega}{\mu_r \mu_0 \omega}\right)^{1/2}. \qquad [6.21]$$

For example at 10 MHz in copper at 293 K, $v = 1290$ m s^{-1}, much less than the speed of sound in copper.

.3 Energy flow and radiation pressure

We saw in section 5.3 that the Poynting vector was $\mathscr{S} = \mathbf{E} \times \mathbf{H}$ in any medium and that the energy density was $u = \frac{1}{2}(\epsilon_r \epsilon_0 E^2 + \mu_r \mu_0 H^2)$ in a linear, isotropic medium. The average Poynting vector in a dielectric at optical frequencies, where n (and hence k) are real, was given by equation [5.42] as:

$$\langle \mathscr{S} \rangle = \frac{1}{2} E_0 H_0 \, \hat{\mathbf{k}}.$$

In a conductor, where the wave number k is complex, the average Poynting vector can be obtained from (exercise 1):

$$\langle \mathscr{S} \rangle = \frac{1}{2} \text{Re} (\mathbf{E} \times \mathbf{H}^*) \qquad [6.22]$$

where Re means 'real part of' and $\mathbf{H}^*$ is the complex conjugate of $\mathbf{H}$, obtained by substituting $-i$ for i.

For a good conductor the electric and magnetic vectors of a plane wave are given by equations [6.16] and [6.17]. The energy density is therefore:

$$u = \frac{1}{2} \left\{ \epsilon_r \epsilon_0 E_0^{\,2} + \mu_r \mu_0 \, (\sigma^2 \delta^2 E_0^{\,2} / 2) \right\}$$

or

$$u = \frac{E_0{}^2}{2} \left\{ \epsilon_r \epsilon_0 + \frac{\sigma}{\omega} \right\} \qquad [6.23]$$

from the definition of δ in equation [6.13]. Hence the ratio of the magnetic to electric energy is $\sigma/(\omega \epsilon_r \epsilon_0)$ and this can be very large, e.g. 10^{11} for 10 MHz waves in copper at 293 K. Similarly the average Poynting vector from equation [6.22] is:

$$\langle \mathscr{S} \rangle = \frac{1}{2} \left(\frac{\sigma}{2\omega \mu_r \mu_0} \right)^{1/2} \exp \left(-\frac{2z}{\delta} \right) E_0{}^2 \hat{\mathbf{k}}. \qquad [6.24]$$

For a radio wave with $E_0 = 0.1$ V m^{-1} in space, which has a intensity of 30 μW m^{-2} from equation [3.36], the intensity in a metal is much greater and at a depth of δ in copper at 1 MHz is about 5 W m^{-2}.

An electromagnetic wave incident on a good conductor from a vacuum exerts a small radiation pressure. This can be deduced from the incident energy density u_i and energy flux $\mathscr{S}_i$ given by equations [3.36] and [3.35]:

$$u_i = \frac{1}{2} \frac{E_i{}^2}{\mu_0 c^2} + \frac{1}{2} \epsilon_0 E_i{}^2 = \epsilon_0 E_i{}^2 \qquad [6.25]$$

$$\mathscr{S}_i = \epsilon_0 c E_i{}^2 = c u_i . \qquad [6.26]$$

At normal incidence there is near perfect *specular reflection* from a plane surface of a good conductor, so that the incident energy flux is totally reversed, giving rise to the radiation pressure p_r, in the direction of the incident Poynting vector. The energy density is equivalent to a momentum p per unit volume at speed c across unit area or

$$u_i = pc$$

which gives a total change of momentum flux $= 2pc$ after reflection and hence a radiation pressure

$$p_r = 2pc = 2u_i = \frac{2\mathscr{S}_i}{c} . \qquad [6.27]$$

If the radiation is diffuse, then on average one-third of the total energy density is associated with normal incidence and so, for *diffuse reflection*,

$$p_r = \frac{2}{3} u_i = \frac{2\mathscr{S}_i}{3c} .$$ [6.28]

The radiation pressure can also be calculated from the Lorentz force due to the magnetic vector acting on the induced surface current in a direction normal to the surface (exercise 2). It is extremely small for sunlight and even for an intense source such as a laser beam, where an intensity of 100 GW m^{-2} produces a radiation pressure of 670 Pa when specularly reflected, it is less than one-hundredth of an atmosphere. However, it is of vital importance in stars, where it prevents a gravitational collapse.

.4 Plasmas

A plasma is an electrically neutral, ionised gas consisting of equal numbers of light electrons and heavy ions. Since the ions have masses at least $m_p = 1836\, m_e$ they are assumed to be stationary and only the electrons are mobile. Here we consider only cold plasmas, that is we neglect the thermal motions of the electrons and ions. Since the simplest model of a metal is the free electron gas, in which the lattice of positive ion cores provides electrical neutrality, a metal can also be regarded as a plasma in its inter-action with electromagnetic radiation.

The current density for N electrons per unit volume each of charge $-e$ and moving with velocity $\mathbf{v}_e$ is:

$$\mathbf{j} = -Ne\, \mathbf{v}_e$$ [6.29]

while their equation of motion in the presence of the electro-magnetic radiation is:

$$m\, \frac{\mathrm{d}\mathbf{v}_e}{\mathrm{d}t} = -e\, (\mathbf{E} + \mathbf{v}_e \times \mathbf{B}) - \frac{m\mathbf{v}_e}{\tau}$$ [6.30]

where the Lorentz force is reduced by the momentum loss in collisions with a mean time τ between collisions. The magnetic force can be neglected, since from equation [6.14] :

$$\frac{|\mathbf{v}_e \times \mathbf{B}|}{\mathbf{E}} \sim \frac{v_e k}{\omega} \sim \frac{v_e}{v}$$

and the phase velocity of the wave v is much greater than the electron velocity v_e. Assuming a frequency dependence $\exp i\omega$ for both $\mathbf{E}$ and $\mathbf{v}_e$, equation [6.30] becomes:

$$\mathbf{v}_e = \frac{-e\mathbf{E}}{m(i\omega + 1/\tau)}$$

and so the current density from equation [6.29] is:

$$\mathbf{j} = \frac{Ne^2 \mathbf{E}\tau}{m(1 + i\omega\tau)}. \qquad [6.31]$$

The wave parameters of the plasma can be described, like those of a dielectric, in terms of a complex refractive index $n = n_R - in_I$, equation [4.29], or a complex permittivity $\epsilon_r = \epsilon_R - i\epsilon_I$, equation [4.32]. The latter follows from Maxwell' fourth equation [1.23]:

$$\text{curl } \mathbf{H} = \mathbf{j}_f + \frac{\partial \mathbf{D}}{\partial t}$$

where in a plasma there is no polarisation and so, using equation [6.31],

$$\frac{Ne^2 \mathbf{E}\tau}{m(1 + i\omega\tau)} + i\omega\epsilon_0 \mathbf{E} = i\omega\epsilon_r\epsilon_0 \mathbf{E}$$

or

$$\epsilon_r = 1 + \frac{Ne^2 \tau}{i\omega m \epsilon_0 (1 + i\omega\tau)}. \qquad [6.32]$$

At *low frequencies* $\omega\tau \ll 1$ and, in a good conductor $\omega \ll \sigma/\epsilon_0$, where $\sigma = Ne^2\tau/m$, so that we have

$$\epsilon_r = -\frac{i\sigma}{\omega\epsilon_0}. \qquad [6.33]$$

For copper at 293 K, $\sigma = 5.8 \times 10^7$ Ω^{-1} m^{-1}, $N = 8.5 \times 10^{28}$ so that $\tau = 2.4 \times 10^{-14}$ s and the limit for $\omega\tau \ll 1$ is a frequency less than 1 THz (millimetre waves). Since the skin depth $\delta = 1/k_I = c/\omega\epsilon_r^{1/2}$ we recover the previous formula $\delta = (2/\mu_0\sigma\omega)^{1/2}$

for a good, paramagnetic conductor like copper.

At *high frequencies* $\omega\tau \gg 1$ and so:

permittivity

$$\epsilon_r = 1 - \frac{Ne^2}{m\epsilon_0 \omega^2} \qquad [6.34]$$

is a real permittivity, giving a real refractive index, which is less than one (as already seen for X-rays in dielectrics, equation [4.37]). The *plasma frequency* ω_p is given by

$$\omega_p{}^2 = Ne^2/m\epsilon_0 \qquad [6.35]$$

so that equation [6.34] can also be written:

$$\epsilon_r = n^2 = \frac{k^2 c^2}{\omega^2} = 1 - \frac{\omega_p{}^2}{\omega^2}$$

or

$$\omega^2 = \omega_p{}^2 + k^2 c^2. \qquad [6.36]$$

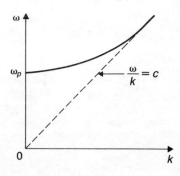

Fig. 6.2 The dispersion relation for high frequency ($\omega\tau \gg 1$) propagation in a plasma with plasma frequency ω_p

This is the dispersion relation for high-frequency propagation in a plasma and is shown in Fig. 6.2. Obviously for $\omega > \omega_p$ there is no attenuation and so a metal at these frequencies becomes transparent. For an alkali metal like sodium, absorption begins in the ultraviolet, but for less-dense plasmas (Table 6.1) the cut-off frequencies are much lower. For example in a gas discharge or a semiconductor with $N = 10^{21}$ m^{-3} the plasma frequency is 300 GHz, while in the ionosphere, with $N = 10^{11}$ m^{-3}, it is only 3 MHz. In the latter case, since the electron density increases with height, medium radio waves ($f < 3$ MHz) are bent back to earth, providing long-distance terrestrial communications, while short waves ($f > 3$ MHz) are necessary for transmissions to satellites beyond the ionosphere.

Chapter 7
Generation of electromagnetic waves

In the last four chapters we have studied the propagation of electromagnetic waves in free space, in dielectrics and in conductors, while ignoring the question of their generation. Now we go back to the *inhomogeneous wave equations* and their solutions the *retarded vector and scalar potentials.* We first develop these potentials for the radiant energy a long way from an oscillating electric dipole and then discuss how the radiators of electromagnetic energy at radio and microwave wavelengths (antennas) can be made directional. Finally we consider the classical scattering of electromagnetic waves.

7.1 Hertzian dipole

We saw in Chapter 2 that when we solved the inhomogeneous wave equations (equations [2.32] and [2.33]) for a distribution of moving charges and currents (Fig. 2.11), we obtained potentials at fixed field points $[1, t] \equiv (x, y, z, t)$ due to the charges and currents at the source points at the earlier time $(t - r_{12}/c)$. In this way the retarded potentials allow for the finite time taken to propagate at speed c:

$$\mathbf{A}(1, t) = \frac{\mu_0}{4\pi} \int \frac{\mathbf{j}(2, t - r_{12}/c)}{r_{12}} d\tau_2 \qquad [2.53]$$

$$\phi(1, t) = \frac{1}{4\pi\epsilon_0} \int \frac{\rho(2, t - r_{12}/c)}{r_{12}} d\tau_2. \qquad [2.54]$$

Having found $\mathbf{A}, \phi$ for a particular source of radiation, the electric and magnetic fields are given by:

$$\mathbf{E} = -\operatorname{grad} \phi - \frac{\partial \mathbf{A}}{\partial t} \qquad [2.29]$$

$$\mathbf{B} = \operatorname{curl} \mathbf{A}. \qquad [2.26]$$

In general the calculation of $\mathbf{A}$, ϕ is complicated for finite sources and so we solve a simple case, the Hertzian (or oscillating) electric dipole. This is an approximation to an oscillator, angular frequency ω, connected to a dipole antenna length l (Fig. 7.1(a)) when $l \ll \lambda$, the wavelength of the radiation.

Potentials

Consider an electric dipole $\mathbf{p} = q\mathbf{l}$ along the z axis and at the origin of a spherical polar coordinate system, Fig. 7.1(b). For an oscillating dipole moment we have

$$q = q_0 \sin \omega t, \mathbf{p} = \mathbf{p}_0 \sin \omega t$$

but for points at a distance $r \gg l$, we may neglect the time taken

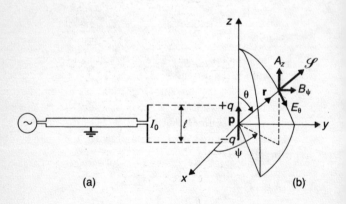

Fig. 7.1 (a) A radio-frequency oscillator connected through a shielded cable to a dipole antenna is equivalent to (b) a Hertzian dipole **p** producing at (r, θ, ψ) a radiant vector potential A_z, electric field E_θ, magnetic field B_ψ and Poynting vector $\mathscr{S} = \mathbf{E} \times \mathbf{B}/\mu_0$

for a signal to traverse the source $(T/2)$ compared with the time (r/c) for propagation to the field point **r**. The current I, given by

$$I = \frac{dq}{dt} = I_0 \cos \omega t \qquad [7.1]$$

where $I_0 = \omega q_0$ is constant across l, is related to the current density **j** for a thin wire by:

$$\mathbf{j}d\tau = I\mathbf{dl}$$

where **dl** is a vector in the direction of the current, here along $0z$. Therefore the dipole **p** generates only the z component of the vector potential **A** and equation [2.53] becomes:

$$A_z(1, t) = \frac{\mu_0}{4\pi} \int \frac{I(2, t - r_{12}/c)}{r_{12}} dl.$$

For a distant point $(r \gg l)$ of a dipole $(\lambda \gg l)$ we may put $r_{12} = |\mathbf{r}_1 - \mathbf{r}_2| \cong r$ and take the integration of the current from $-l/2$ to $+l/2$, so that

$$A_z(r, t) = \left(\frac{\mu_0 l}{4\pi}\right) \frac{I(t - r/c)}{r}. \qquad [7.2]$$

Thus **A** is everywhere parallel to **p**, Fig. 7.1(b), and decreases as $1/r$, as expected for a spherical wave (see equation [3.23]).

The scalar potential can be found most easily from the Lorentz condition:

$$\text{div } \mathbf{A} = -\frac{1}{c^2} \frac{\partial \phi}{\partial t} \qquad [2.31]$$

where here:

$$\text{div } \mathbf{A} = \frac{\partial A_z}{\partial z} = \left(\frac{\mu_0 l}{4\pi}\right) \frac{\partial}{\partial z} \left\{\frac{I(t - r/c)}{r}\right\}. \qquad [7.3]$$

The solution for ϕ, after differentiating the product and integrating the time derivative (exercise 1), is

$$\phi = \frac{l}{4\pi\epsilon_0} \left\{\frac{\cos \theta}{r^2} \cdot q(t - r/c) + \frac{\cos \theta}{cr} I(t - r/c)\right\} \qquad [7.4]$$

where $q(t - r/c) = q_0 \sin \omega(t - r/c)$ and $I(t - r/c) = \omega q_0 \cos \omega(t - r/c)$.

Fields

From equations [2.26] and [7.2], the magnetic field

$$\mathbf{B} = \mathrm{curl}\, \mathbf{A} = \frac{\mu_0}{4\pi}\, \mathrm{curl}\left\{ \frac{I(t - r/c)}{r}\, \mathbf{l} \right\}$$

and, using the vector identity for the curl of a product (Appendix 4), we have

$$\mathbf{B} = \frac{\mu_0}{4\pi}\left[\frac{I(t - r/c)}{r}\, \mathrm{curl}\, \mathbf{l} + \mathrm{grad}\left\{ \frac{I(t - r/c)}{r} \right\} \times \mathbf{l} \right].$$

But $\mathrm{curl}\, \mathbf{l} = 0$, since $\mathbf{l}$ is along $0z$, and I varies in space only with $\mathbf{r}$, so that:

$$\mathbf{B} = \frac{\mu_0}{4\pi}\left[\mathbf{l} \times \frac{\partial}{\partial r}\left\{ \frac{I_0 \cos \omega (t - r/c)}{r} \right\} \hat{\mathbf{r}} \right]. \qquad [7.5]$$

Therefore $\mathbf{B}$ is normal to both $\mathbf{l}$ and $\mathbf{r}$ and so must be tangentia to an azimuthal circle, that is, $\mathbf{B} = B_\psi\, \hat{\boldsymbol{\psi}}$. Since $\mathbf{l} \times \hat{\mathbf{r}} = l \sin \theta$ equation [7.5] becomes:

$$B_\psi = \left(\frac{\mu_0 l I_0 \sin \theta}{4\pi} \right) \frac{\cos \omega (t - r/c)}{r^2}$$

$$- \left(\frac{\mu_0 \omega l I_0 \sin \theta}{4\pi c} \right) \frac{\sin \omega (t - r/c)}{r}. \qquad [7.6]$$

This expression shows the general result for the electromagneti field due to changing currents. It consists of two terms.

1. A term decreasing more rapidly than $1/r$ – the *induction* (o near) *field*.
2. A term decreasing as $1/r$ – the *radiation* (or far) *field*.

The induction field dominates when $r \ll \lambda$ and in this case is jus the field given by the law of Biot and Savart, equation [2.44] that we found by taking curl $\mathbf{A}$ for a circuit $\oint I\mathbf{dl}$. If we draw sphere of large radius round the dipole the total energy into i is given by $\int \mathscr{S}.\mathbf{dS}$ over the surface of the sphere, so that th contribution to this integral of field terms that decrease mor rapidly than $1/r$ tend to zero for a sphere of large enough radius Hence in calculating the *radiant* energy we include only th *radiation field* term, which decreases as $1/r$.

In a similar way the electric radiation field E_θ is found in spherical polar coordinates from equations [2.29], [7.2] and [7.4] to be (exercise 2):

$$E_\theta = -\left(\frac{\omega l I_0 \sin\theta}{4\pi\epsilon_0 c^2}\right)\frac{\sin\omega(t-r/c)}{r} \qquad [7.7]$$

i.e. normal to $\hat{r}$ and B_ψ, as shown in Fig. 7.1(b). In amplitude the ratio

$$\frac{E_\theta}{B_\psi} = \frac{1}{\mu_0\epsilon_0 c} = c \qquad [7.8]$$

for spherical waves in space, as was found for plane waves (equation [3.18]). The electric-field lines in the axial plane are plotted in Fig. 7.2(a); they have cylindrical symmetry about the dipole axis. Both the electric and magnetic vectors vary as $\sin\theta$ in amplitude, as shown in Fig. 7.2(b) by the dashed circles.

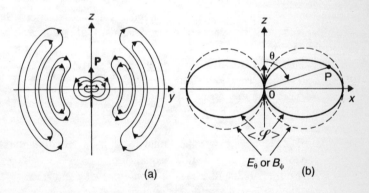

Fig. 7.2 (a) The electric field lines in the axial plane of the Hertzian dipole for $\omega t = 0$, 2π, 4π ... The pattern is the same for $\omega t = \pi$, 3π, 5π, but with all the directions reversed. The magnetic field lines are azimuthal circles about the vertical axis of the dipole. (b) Polar plots of the amplitude of the electric E_θ and magnetic B_ψ fields (---) and of the average Poynting vector $\langle\mathscr{S}\rangle$ (——) for a Hertzian dipole. The radiant energy in the direction θ is proportional to the length OP and independent of the azimuthal angle ψ, so that in three dimensions the polar plot has a doughnut shape with no radiation along the axis and a maximum in the equatorial plane

7.2 Radiant energy and power

The radiant energy crossing unit area per second, the energy flux (or Poynting) vector, is in free space

$$\mathscr{S} = \mathbf{E} \times \mathbf{B}/\mu_0 \qquad [3.31]$$

which gives for the Hertzian dipole

$$\mathscr{S} = \left\{ -\frac{E_0}{r} \sin \omega \, (t - r/c) \, \hat{\boldsymbol{\theta}} \right\} \times - \left\{ \frac{E_0}{\mu_0 cr} \sin \omega \, (t - r/c) \, \hat{\boldsymbol{\psi}} \right\}$$

where $E_0 = (\omega l I_0 \sin \theta)/(4\pi\epsilon_0 c^2)$. Since $\hat{\boldsymbol{\theta}} \times \hat{\boldsymbol{\psi}} = \hat{\mathbf{r}}$, $\mathscr{S}$ is a radial vector, (Fig. 7.1(b)) as expected for a spherical wave, and

$$\mathscr{S} = \left(\frac{E_0^2}{\mu_0 cr^2} \right) \sin^2 \omega \, (t - r/c) \, \hat{\mathbf{r}}. \qquad [7.9]$$

The time-averaged Poynting vector is, therefore (exercise 2),

$$\langle \mathscr{S} \rangle = \left(\frac{\mu_0 c l^2}{32\pi^2} \right) I_0^2 \sin^2 \theta \, \frac{k^2}{r^2} \, \hat{\mathbf{r}} \qquad [7.10]$$

where $k = \omega/c$ is the wave number for the radiation. Since $\langle \mathscr{S} \rangle$ is axially symmetrical (independent of ψ) it is usually drawn on a polar plot (Fig. 7.2(b)), which is a vertical section of a doughnut-shaped surface. Its polar variation is as $\sin^2 \theta$, so that there is no radiation along the axis of the dipole ($\theta = 0$) and a maximum output in the equatorial plane ($\theta = \pi/2$). As expected $\langle \mathscr{S} \rangle$ is proportional to $1/r^2$ so that the energy flow through any solid angle is the same for all r. Since $\langle \mathscr{S} \rangle$ varies as $l^2 I_0^2 k^2$, which is proportional to $\omega^4 p_0^2$, radiation is much more efficient at high source frequencies.

The total radiated power W is obtained by integrating $\langle \mathscr{S} \rangle$ over the surface of a sphere of radius r, that is

$$W = \int_S \langle \mathscr{S} \rangle . \mathbf{dS}$$

where $dS = r \sin \theta \, d\psi r d\theta$.

Hence:

$$W = \left(\frac{\mu_0 c l^2 I_0^2 k^2}{32\pi^2} \right) \int_0^\pi \left(\frac{\sin^2 \theta}{r^2} \right) r^2 \sin \theta \, d\theta \int_0^{2\pi} d\psi,$$

or

$$W = (\mu_0 c l^2 I_0{}^2 k^2)/12\pi. \qquad [7.11]$$

This power is conveniently expressed as:

$$W = \frac{1}{2} R_r I_0{}^2 \qquad [7.12]$$

where R_r is the *radiation resistance* of the source, since this is just the mean power that would be dissipated in a resistor whose $I^2{}_{rms} = I_0{}^2/2$. For the Hertzian dipole

$$R_r = \frac{\mu_0 c l^2 k^2}{6\pi} = 20(kl)^2 \qquad [7.13]$$

and so depends only on the ratio l/λ, which we have assumed to be small. Thus a dipole antenna can be matched quite easily to a low impedance shielded cable (Fig. 7.1 (a)).

7.3 Antennas

The principles that we have used to calculate the electromagnetic field, the radiated power and the radiation resistance for the Hertzian dipole can also be applied to other sources of radiation, such as microscopic sources (magnetic dipoles and electric quadrupoles) and macroscopic sources (radio antennas).

Microscopic sources

A magnetic dipole in the form of a current loop of area $dS = \pi a^2$ has magnetic moment,

$$\mathbf{m}_0 = I \mathbf{dS} \qquad [7.14]$$

where $\mathbf{m}_0$ is along $0z$ for a current loop in the xy plane. For an oscillating dipole moment,

$$m = m_0 \cos \omega t, \qquad [7.15]$$

the electromagnetic field can be shown to be similar to that for the electric dipole, Fig. 7.1(b), except that B_ψ is now replaced by E_ψ and E_θ is replaced by $-B_\theta$, thus keeping $\mathscr{S}$ along $\mathbf{r}$ at a distance point $r \gg a$ for wavelengths $\lambda \gg a$. For a small loop the scalar potential ϕ will be constant and can be set to zero, so that both of the components of the electromagnetic field are due to the magnetic vector potential $\mathbf{A}$. They can be shown to be:

$$E_\psi = \left(\frac{\mu_0 \omega^2 m_0 \sin \theta}{4\pi c}\right) \frac{\cos \omega (t - r/c)}{r} \qquad [7.16]$$

and

$$-B_\theta = \left(\frac{\mu_0 \omega^2 m_0 \sin \theta}{4\pi c^2}\right) \frac{\cos \omega (t - r/c)}{r} \qquad [7.17]$$

so that again $|\mathbf{E}/\mathbf{B}| = c$ and the time-averaged Poynting vector is

$$\langle \mathscr{S} \rangle = \left(\frac{\mu_0 c m_0^2}{32\pi^2}\right) \sin^2 \theta \left(\frac{k^4}{r^2}\right) \hat{\mathbf{r}}. \qquad [7.18]$$

Comparing this with equation [7.10] we see that $\langle \mathscr{S} \rangle$ is now proportional to $\omega^4 m_0^2$ rather than $\omega^4 p_0^2$. The corresponding radiation resistance (exercise 4) is $20\pi^2 (ka)^4$.

A linear electric quadrupole can be formed by placing two dipoles end-on so that their negative charges coincide, Fig. 7.3(a). It has a quadrupole moment $Q_{zz} = \sum_i q z_i^2 = 2ql^2$ and if each charge q oscillates in amplitude as $q_0 \cos \omega t$, then the quadrupole moment is

$$Q_{zz} = Q_0 \cos \omega t \qquad [7.19]$$

where $Q_0 = 2q_0 l^2$. Considering only the radiation field, we can find its field components by superimposing the dipole fields of electric dipoles centred at $z = \pm l/2$, after allowing for their phase difference. The resultant fields are:

$$E_\theta = \left(-\frac{\mu_0 \omega^3 Q_0 \sin \theta \cos \theta}{8\pi c}\right) \frac{\cos \omega (t - r/c)}{r} \qquad [7.20]$$

$$B_\psi = -\left(\frac{\mu_0 \omega^3 Q_0 \sin \theta \cos \theta}{8\pi c^2}\right) \frac{\cos \omega (t - r/c)}{r}. \qquad [7.21]$$

There can be no radiation along the directions $\theta = 0, \pi$, since these are the dipole axes, nor along $\theta = \pi/2$, where the dipole

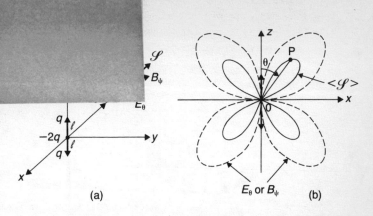

Fig. 7.3 (a) A linear electric quadrupole and its radiation field. (b) Polar plots of the amplitude of the electric and magnetic fields (---) and of the average Poynting vector (—) for a linear quadrupole. The plots are independent of ψ

fields cancel. The field patterns are therefore given by the dashed curve in Fig. 7.3(b) and the polar diagram for $\langle\mathscr{S}\rangle$, which varies as $\sin^2 \theta \cos^2 \theta$, is the solid curve. It is noticeable that the fields now vary as $\omega^3 Q_0$ and the power as $\omega^6 Q_0^2$, giving a radiation resistance (exercise 5) of $4 (kl)^4$

Macroscopic sources

Most sources of radio waves use a half-wave ($\lambda/2$) antenna, Fig. 7.4(a), or a combination of $\lambda/2$ antennas. In the $\lambda/2$ antenna the current is:

$$I = I_0 \cos (kl) \cos \omega t \qquad [7.22]$$

where l is now a variable and each current element $I\mathbf{dl}$ acts as an electric dipole producing a radiation field, from equation [7.7], of:

$$dE_\theta = - \left(\frac{\omega dlI_0 \cos (kl) \sin \theta'}{4\pi\epsilon_0 c^2} \right) \frac{\sin \omega (t - r'/c)}{r'} \qquad [7.23]$$

where $\mathbf{r}'$, θ' are shown on Fig. 7.4(a). The total field is given by the coherent superposition of these dipole fields with $r' \approx r - l \cos \theta$, $\sin \theta'/r' \approx \sin \theta/r$, but with the phase differences retained, so that:

$$E_\theta = -\frac{\omega I_0}{4\pi\epsilon_0 c^2} \int_{-\lambda/4}^{\lambda/4} \frac{\cos(kl)\sin\theta \sin\omega(t - r'/c)}{r}\, \mathrm{d}l.$$

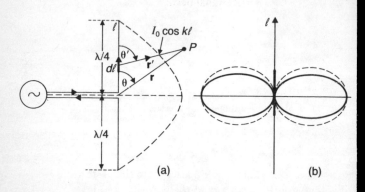

Fig. 7.4 (a) Half-wave antenna and its current distribution at $t = 0$. (b) Polar diagrams of the radiation fields (---) and radiant energy flux from a half-wave antenna

Calculation shows that:

$$E_\theta = \frac{I_0}{2\pi\epsilon_0 c} \cdot \frac{\cos\left(\dfrac{\pi}{2}\cos\theta\right)}{\sin\theta} \cdot \sin\omega(t - r/c) \qquad [7.24]$$

and that

$$B_\psi = E_0/c \qquad [7.25]$$

as with the dipole. The resultant field and energy-flux polar diagram, Fig. 7.4(b), is very similar to that of the dipole, Fig. 7.2(b), but the $\lambda/2$ antenna is slightly more directional. On the other hand the fields are now independent of the frequency for a given current, unlike the dipole fields, following the integration over $\lambda/2$.

A simple way to make a directional antenna is to place two $\lambda/2$ antennas $\lambda/4$ apart, Fig. 7.5(a), and to supply them with equal currents $\pi/2$ out of time phase. The coherent superposition of the radiation fields then produces almost perfect cancellation in one direction and an enhanced energy flux in the other, as shown for the plane normal to the antennas in Fig. 7.5(b). At higher frequencies (smaller wavelengths) a parabolic reflector with the source at its focus produces a parallel beam, Fig. 7.6(a), while at microwave frequencies a waveguide horn, Fig. 7.6(b), gives a highly directional beam.

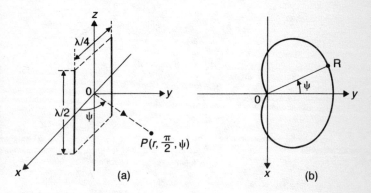

Fig. 7.5 (a) Two half-wave antennas spaced $\lambda/4$ apart and with currents $\pi/2$ out of phase. (b) Polar diagram of these antennas for radiant energy flux in the azimuthal plane, where the flux in direction ψ is proportional to OR

Application of the *reciprocity theorem*, well-known in network theory, to a pair of antennas shows that the current in a receiving antenna divided by the voltage at the transmitting antenna remains constant when the source and detector are interchanged, provided all the impedances and frequency are constant. This is a valuable aid in designing antennas, since it means that the polar diagram of a transmitting antenna is the same as the polar response of the same antenna used as a receiver.

7.4 Scattering

When electromagnetic radiation interacts with a charge distribution, such as a molecule, the resultant motion of the charges becomes a secondary source. This process is termed *scattering* of the incident radiation. We consider here the elastic scattering of the radiation from oscillating charges at non-relativistic speeds.

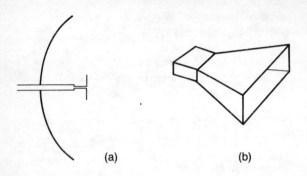

Fig. 7.6 Directional antennas: (a) parabolic reflector with half-wave dipole at its focus to produce a parallel beam; (b) pyramidal horn ('cheese') antenna at end of a waveguide for a microwave beam

The total radiated power W of a Hertzian dipole, equation [7.11], can be expressed more generally (exercise 6) in terms of the second derivative of the dipole moment, evaluated at the retarded time $(t - r/c)$:

$$[\ddot{\mathbf{p}}] = \omega^2 \, [\mathbf{p}] \qquad [7.26]$$

as

$$W = [\ddot{\mathbf{p}}]^2 / (6\pi\epsilon_0 c^3) \qquad [7.27]$$

which is known as *Larmor's formula*. We can apply this to both bound and free electrons.

For bound electrons we have an electric dipole polarisability $\alpha\,(\omega)$, equation [4.8], and a displacement x given by equations [4.4] and [4.6]:

$$x = \frac{-eE_0 \exp\,(i\omega t)}{m\,({\omega_0}^2 - \omega^2 + i\omega\gamma)} \qquad [7.28]$$

where ω_0 is the natural frequency and γ the damping constant of the oscillating electrons. The instantaneous dipole moment is:

$$\mathbf{p} = -e\mathbf{x} \qquad [7.29]$$

and so, from equations [7.27], [7.28] and [7.29], the power radiated by the oscillating electron is:

$$W = \frac{e^4 E_0{}^2 \omega^2}{12\pi\epsilon_0 m^2 c^3 \; \{(\omega^2{}_0 - \omega^2)^2 + \omega^2\gamma^2\}} \qquad [7.30]$$

The *scattering cross-section* σ is the ratio of the radiated power to the power per unit area in the incident beam, from equation [3.36]:

$$\langle \mathscr{S} \rangle = \frac{1}{2}\epsilon_0 c E_0{}^2. \qquad [7.31]$$

Hence:

$$\sigma = \frac{W}{\langle \mathscr{S} \rangle} = \frac{8\pi r_0{}^2}{3} \; \frac{\omega^4}{\{(\omega_0{}^2 - \omega^2)^2 + \omega^2\gamma^2\}} \qquad [7.32]$$

where

$$r_0 = \frac{e^2}{4\pi\epsilon_0 mc^2} \qquad [7.33]$$

is the *classical electron radius*, about 2.8 fm.

The frequency dependence of this cross-section is shown in Fig. 7.7. At low frequencies, $\omega \ll \omega_0$, and since $\gamma \ll \omega_0$, the cross-section becomes:

$$\sigma_R = \frac{8\pi r_0{}^2}{3} \left(\frac{\omega}{\omega_0}\right)^4 \qquad [7.34]$$

which is the *Rayleigh scattering law*. It shows that scattering varies as λ^{-4} and so short wavelengths are scattered much more than long wavelengths. A familiar example is the sky: blue in the day due to scattered sunlight, but red at sunrise and sunset when seen in the reflection of the sun's rays from high clouds.

When the frequency of the incident radiation is the same as the natural frequency of the oscillating electrons, the induced dipole moment is very large and the scattered radiation peaks at

ω_0. This is known as *resonant scattering*, or resonance fluorescence in quantum theory, and produces a Lorentzian shaped line of amplitude:

$$\sigma_0 = \frac{8\pi r_0^2}{3} \left(\frac{\omega_0}{\omega}\right)^2. \qquad [7.35]$$

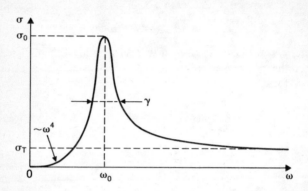

Fig. 7.7 Cross-section for elastic scattering of radiation by a molecule with electronic oscillators of natural frequency ω_0 and damping constant γ. For $\omega \ll \omega_0$ there is Rayleigh scattering and for $\omega \gg \omega_0$ there is Thomson scattering, cross-section σ_T

At the highest frequencies, $\omega \gg \omega_0$, $\gamma \ll \omega_0$, the electron is effectively free, and its displacement becomes:

$$x = \frac{eE_0}{m\omega^2} \exp(i\omega t)$$

and the cross-section is just:

$$\sigma_T = \frac{8\pi r_0^2}{3}. \qquad [7.36]$$

This is *Thomson scattering* of free electrons and has a very small cross-section, from equation [7.33], of only 6.6×10^{-29} m². Only electrons in a dense plasma are likely to produce significant Thomson scattering, one example being the corona seen round the sun as a bright ring during a total eclipse of the sun. In terms of σ_T we see that:

$$\frac{\sigma_R}{\sigma_T} = \left(\frac{\omega}{\omega_0}\right)^4 \text{ and } \frac{\sigma_0}{\sigma_T} = \left(\frac{\omega_0}{\gamma}\right)^2 \qquad [7.37]$$

At still higher frequencies classical theory no longer applies and we get photon–electron collisions or Compton scattering. The classical limit is $\hbar\omega \ll mc^2$ for Thomson scattering, from quantum theory.

Chapter 8
Guided waves

In this chapter we consider first the difference between free space and guided waves and then develop the theory for electromagnetic waves in rectangular waveguides. A discussion of waveguide modes is followed by an introduced to resonant cavities and the chapter concludes with the shortcomings of the classical theory of cavity radiation.

8.1 Waveguide equation

A familiar experience when driving with a car radio on is to find the broadcast signal cut out within a short tunnel, although the end of the tunnel can be clearly seen in daylight. In such circumstances the tunnel is probably lined with steel-reinforced concrete and the mesh of steel wires forms a waveguide which evidently will not pass radio waves. Why should this waveguide pass electromagnetic waves at optical wavelengths but not at radio ones? An elegant answer to this question, due to Feynmann, is to consider a line source S between two infinite, parallel plane conductors (Fig. 8.1(a)) spaced a apart. We know from the method of images in electrostatics that conductors act like mirrors in computing the resultant electric field, and the same is true for electrodynamics. The source S and the reflecting waveguide can therefore be replaced by a doubly infinite set of images $1, 1', 1'' \ldots, 2, 2', 2'' \ldots$ (Fig. 8.1(b)). If the initial phase of S is positive then the initial phase of the images 1, 2 will be negative, of the images $1'$ and $2'$ will be positive, etc., so that the fields are zero at the mirrors, that is at the conducting walls.

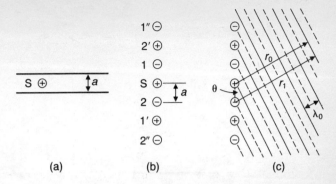

Fig. 8.1 (a) A line source S placed between two infinite, parallel plane conductors is equivalent to (b) a source S plus multiple images 1, 1′, 1″ . . . , 2, 2′, 2″ . . . in the conductors, which radiate (c) coherently in direction $(\theta + \pi/2)$

The resultant superposition of waves can be calculated from the *retarded* potentials, equations [2.53] and [2.54], and will produce both near and far fields, as did the Hertzian dipole, equation [7.6]. For the source S and its images these fields all cancel, but the far fields depend on the direction of propagation. For those directions in which all the fields are *in phase*, the fields will be strong and propagate as plane waves (Fig. 8.1(c)) so that:

$$r_1 - r_0 = \lambda_0/2$$

and

$$\sin \theta = \lambda_0/2a. \qquad [8.1]$$

By symmetry, a similar set must propagate at $-\theta$ and when these two are superimposed we get the complete fields.

In Fig. 8.2 we have used the image construction to draw the plane waves within the waveguide and we see that the wave pattern goes from a double trough at P to a double crest at Q to a double trough at R, etc., at a phase velocity v. The *waveguide wavelength* is therefore λ_g, which is clearly longer than the free-space wavelength λ_0, since:

$$\lambda_0 = \lambda_g \cos \theta. \qquad [8.2]$$

However, from equation [8.1]

$$\cos^2 \theta = 1 - (\lambda_0/2a)^2 \qquad [8.3]$$

so that

$$\frac{1}{{\lambda_0}^2} = \frac{1}{{\lambda_g}^2} + \frac{1}{(2a)^2} \cdot \qquad [8.4]$$

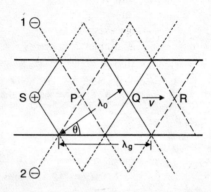

Fig. 8.2 The wave in the waveguide is formed by the superposition of the coherent radiations from the image sources and has a wavelength $\lambda_g > \lambda_0$, the free space wavelength

Now we can see that if λ_0 is a long wavelength, greater than $2a$, it is impossible to find an angle θ for propagation. Therefore the constructive interference of the reflected waves, which allows the signal to travel down the guide, only occurs for wavelengths $\lambda_0 < 2a$. For this waveguide of two infinite conducting planes, the *cut-off wavelength* $\lambda_c = 2a$ and equation [8.4] becomes:

$$\frac{1}{{\lambda_0}^2} = \frac{1}{{\lambda_g}^2} + \frac{1}{{\lambda_c}^2} \qquad [8.5]$$

which is known as the waveguide equation.

8.2 Rectangular waveguides

For microwaves and millimetre waves the common shape for a

waveguide is rectangular. It also has the simplest equations for its electric and magnetic fields, which we will now derive.

Electric field

A typical waveguide is shown in Fig. 8.3(a), where the widths are $x = a, y = b$ with $a \approx 2b$, and the wave propagates along z. The field vectors $\mathbf{E}$ and $\mathbf{B}$ of this wave must satisfy Maxwell's equations, but there are many possible solutions, or *waveguide modes*, for propagating waves that satisfy the boundary conditions (see section 5.1). The simplest mode for this rectangular waveguide is a wave with the electric field everywhere transverse (E_y): it is a TE mode. In lowest order it must be zero at $x = 0$ and $x = a$, since there is no tangential component of $\mathbf{E}$ at the surface of a conductor, and will have a maximum in the centre (Fig. 8.3(b)) so that

$$E_y = E_0 \sin k_x x \qquad [8.6]$$

where $k_x = 2\pi/2a$. If the wave travels with a phase velocity $v = \omega/k_g$, where $k_g = 2\pi/\lambda_g$, then, as in Fig. 8.3(c)

$$E_y = E_0 \sin k_x x \exp i\,(\omega t - k_g z) \qquad [8.7]$$

where k_g must satisfy Maxwell's equations.

Since $\partial E_y/\partial y = 0$, E_y satisfies div $\mathbf{E} = 0$, equation [1.5]. The other Maxwell equations lead to (section 3.1):

$$\nabla^2 \mathbf{E} = \frac{1}{c^2} \frac{\partial^2 E}{\partial t^2} \qquad [8.8]$$

where here $\mathbf{E} = 0\hat{\mathbf{i}} + E_y\hat{\mathbf{j}} + 0\hat{\mathbf{k}}$. From equations [8.6] and [8.7]:

$$\nabla^2 \mathbf{E} = -k_x^2 E_y + 0 - k_g^2 E_y$$

and

$$\partial^2 E_y/\partial t^2 = -\omega^2 E_y$$

so that

$$k_x^2 + k_g^2 = \omega^2/c^2. \qquad [8.9]$$

Since $k_x = 2\pi/2a$ for this fundamental mode, this can be rearranged as:

$$\frac{1}{(2a)^2} + \frac{1}{\lambda_g{}^2} = \frac{1}{\lambda_0{}^2}$$

and we recover equation [8.4] for the guide wavelength.

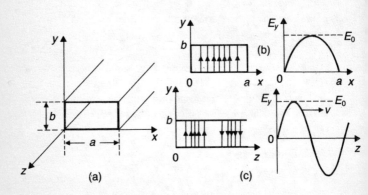

Fig. 8.3 (a) Rectangular waveguide, $x = a$, $y = b$. (b) Simple transverse electric (TE) mode. (c) Wave travels with phase velocity v along the wave-guide (at $t = 2\pi/4\omega$)

Attenuated wave

In section 8.1 we found that λ_0 had a maximum value $\lambda_c = 2a$, the cut-off wavelength. If we try and propagate a wave with $\lambda_0 > \lambda_c$, or $\omega_0 < \pi c/a$, then equation [8.9] shows that k_g becomes imaginary, as we found for a wave travelling into a conductor (section 6.1). Evidently the wave decays in amplitude as it enters the guide and for $\lambda_0 \gg \lambda_c$ this happens quite rapidly (Fig. 8.4) where $k_g = ik_I$ and equation [8.7] becomes:

$$E_y = E_0 \sin k_x x \exp i\,(\omega t - k_I z). \qquad [8.10]$$

From equation [8.9] when $\lambda_0 \gg \lambda_c = 2a$, $k_I = \pi/a$ and the wave penetrates only a distance a/π (Fig. 8.4) before its amplitude falls to E_0/e.

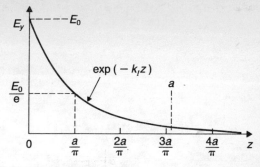

Fig. 8.4 A wave whose wavelength $\lambda_0 \gg \lambda_c$ is rapidly attenuated inside the waveguide and does not propagate

Travelling wave

The phase velocity of a propagating wave is, from equation [8.9]

$$v = \frac{\omega}{k_g} = \frac{1}{\left(\dfrac{1}{c^2} - \dfrac{k_x^{\,2}}{\omega^2} \right)^{1/2}}$$

and for the lowest mode, where $k_x = 2\pi/2a = 2\pi/\lambda_c = \omega_c/c$,

$$v = c / \{ 1 - (\omega_c/\omega)^2 \}^{1/2}. \qquad [8.11]$$

For a travelling wave $\lambda < \lambda_c$ or $\omega > \omega_c$, so the *phase velocity is always greater than c*. However, the group velocity $u = \mathrm{d}\omega/\mathrm{d}k_g$ is not, since it is easily shown to be

$$u = c \{ 1 - (\omega_c/\omega)^2 \}^{1/2} \qquad [8.12]$$

and for all $\omega > \omega_c$, $u < c$. From equations [8.11] and [8.12] we get the important result:

$$vu = c^2. \qquad [8.13]$$

Magnetic field

The magnetic field for this fundamental TE mode is found from the third Maxwell equation:

$$\text{curl } \mathbf{E} = - \partial\mathbf{B}/\partial t. \qquad [1.3]$$

Since $\mathbf{E} = E_y \hat{\mathbf{j}}$, the curl has only two finite components, so that:

$$-\partial E_y/\partial z \; \hat{\mathbf{i}} = -\partial B_x/\partial t \; \hat{\mathbf{i}}$$
$$+\partial E_y/\partial x \; \hat{\mathbf{k}} = -\partial B_z/\partial t \; \hat{\mathbf{k}}$$

and $B_y = 0$. Substituting for E_y from equation [8.7] and putting $k_x = \pi/a$, we obtain:

$$B_x = -\frac{k_g}{\omega} E_0 \sin \frac{\pi x}{a} \exp i\,(\omega t - k_g z) = -\frac{k_g}{\omega} E_y \qquad [8.14]$$

$$B_z = \frac{i\pi}{a\omega} E_0 \cos \frac{\pi x}{a} \exp i\,(\omega t - k_g z) \qquad [8.15]$$

and

$$\frac{B_x}{B_z} = +\frac{ik_g a}{\pi} \frac{\sin \pi x/a}{\cos \pi x/a}. \qquad [8.16]$$

The electric and magnetic fields for this fundamental TE mode are drawn in Fig. 8.5 and we see that the $\mathbf{B}$ field forms loops which, by equation [8.16], are Lissajous figures for the combination of two sine waves that are of unequal amplitude and $\pi/2$ out of phase, i.e. ellipses. They are also, by equation [8.15], centred $\pi/2$ out of phase with the maximum of E_y.

Energy flow

From equations [8.7] and [8.14] the Poynting vector

$$\mathscr{S} = \mathbf{E} \times \mathbf{B}/\mu_0 = E_y \hat{\mathbf{j}} \times B_x \hat{\mathbf{i}}/\mu_0$$

becomes

$$\langle \mathscr{S} \rangle = k_g E_0{}^2 \sin^2\,(\pi x/a)\, \hat{\mathbf{k}}/(2\omega\mu_0). \qquad [8.17]$$

The total power is therefore

$$W = \frac{k_g E_0{}^2}{2\omega\mu_0} \int_0^a \sin^2\left(\frac{\pi x}{a}\right) b \; \mathrm{d}x$$

since $\langle \mathscr{S} \rangle$ is independent of y. Putting $v = \omega/k_g$, we find:

$$W = \frac{1}{4} E_0{}^2 \, ab/\mu_0 v. \qquad\qquad [8.18]$$

It is easy to show (exercise 1) that this power is just the electromagnetic energy per unit length multiplied by u, where u is the group (or signal) velocity given by $u = c^2/v$.

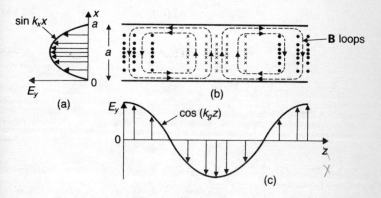

Fig. 8.5 Electric and magnetic fields of a propagating wave in the fundamental TE mode: (a) end view; (b) central section; (c) side view

We have ignored waveguide losses by assuming perfectly conducting walls. In practice high-quality waveguides have a thin coating of silver or gold and a very small attenuation, for example $0.1 \, \mathrm{dB \, m^{-1}}$ at 10 GHz, so that this loss is only significant over long distances.

8.3 Waveguide modes

There is an infinite number of possible modes of propagation of electromagnetic waves in waveguides, but they can be classified into three basic types:

1. transverse electric (TE);
2. transverse magnetic (TM); and
3. transverse electric and magnetic (TEM).

Transverse electric modes

We have already seen that the fundamental (or dominant) TE mode in a rectangular waveguide has one component of $\mathbf{E}$ (E_y) only, but two components of $\mathbf{B}$ (B_x, B_z), producing the field distributions shown in Fig. 8.5. Higher-order TE modes have wave numbers:

$$k_x = m\frac{\pi}{a}, \quad k_y = n\frac{\pi}{b} \qquad [8.19]$$

for a TE_{mn} mode. The fields for such a higher-order mode must satisfy the boundary conditions and Maxwell's equations and it is easily shown using $(t, z) \equiv (\omega t - k_g z)$ that they are:

$$E_x = E_{0x} \cos k_x x \sin k_y y \exp i\,(t, z)$$

$$E_y = E_{0y} \sin k_x x \cos k_y y \exp i\,(t, z)$$

$$E_z = 0$$

$$B_x = B_{0x} \sin k_x x \cos k_y y \exp i\,(t, z)$$

$$B_y = B_{0y} \cos k_x x \sin k_y y \exp i\,(t, z)$$

$$B_z = B_{0z} \cos k_x x \cos k_y y \exp i\,(t, z) \qquad [8.20]$$

where the coefficients E_{0x}, E_{0y}, B_{0x}, B_{0y}, B_{0z} are independent of x, y and z. The cut-off frequency is determined by substituting E_x or E_y into the wave equation [8.8], as before, giving a revised equation [8.9]:

$$k_x^2 + k_y^2 + k_g^2 = \omega^2/c^2. \qquad [8.21]$$

Therefore, from equation [8.19], the cut-off wave number is given by:

$$k_c^2 = \frac{m^2\pi^2}{a^2} + \frac{n^2\pi^2}{b^2}$$

and so the cut-off frequency is:

$$(v_c)_{m,n} = \frac{c}{2}\left(\frac{m^2}{a^2} + \frac{n^2}{b^2}\right)^{1/2}. \qquad [8.22]$$

Transverse magnetic modes

For these modes the magnetic fields are everywhere transverse to the direction of propagation ($0z$), and the electric field consists of longitudinal loops. The boundary conditions require $E_z = 0$ at $x = 0$ and $y = 0$, so

$$E_z = E_{0z} \sin k_x x \sin k_y y \exp i\,(\omega t - k_g z) \qquad [8.23]$$

and the other terms can be found from Maxwell's equations and the boundary conditions, B_z being zero by definition. The resultant TM_{mn} modes have cut-off frequencies given by equation [8.22], but the lowest mode is TM_{11} and there are no TM_{m0} or TM_{0n} modes, as is easily seen from equation [8.23]. This is important in enabling one to choose a waveguide which, for a particular frequency of radiation, will then propagate *only one mode*, the TE_{10} mode (see exercise 2).

Transverse electric and magnetic modes

These modes have no longitudinal electric or magnetic fields and so cannot satisfy the boundary conditions for a closed, conducting waveguide. However, the 'parallel plate' waveguide of section 8.1 is bounded in one direction only and so can propagate TEM waves. The equations for propagation down a coaxial cable are normally developed from distributed capacitance and inductance formulae, but an alternative approach is to regard the wave propagating in the space between the inner diameter and outer diameter of a coaxial line as similar to that in a parallel-plate waveguide folded round into a concentric cylinder with radial distance a between the inner and outer walls (Fig. 8.6(a)). The electric field is then radial, the magnetic field azimuthal and the energy flows along $0z$ (Fig. 8.6(b)) where:

$$\mathscr{S} = E_r \hat{\mathbf{r}} \times B_\theta \hat{\theta} = \mathscr{S}_z \hat{\mathbf{z}} \qquad [8.24]$$

in cylindrical polar coordinates (r, θ, z).

The TEM mode is the one that propagates in free space (see Fig. 3.6) and is the limiting case for a very short wavelength source (e.g. light) propagating between the parallel plates of

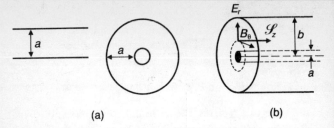

Fig. 8.6 (a) A parallel-plate waveguide wraps round into a coaxial line.
(b) The electric and magnetic fields of a TEM wave in a coaxial cable are
E_r and B_θ

the waveguide of Fig. 8.6(a). Then, from equation [8.2], as
$\lambda_0 \ll 2a$, $\cos \theta \to 1$ and $\lambda \to \lambda_0$. The waveguide ceases to influence
the propagating wave, which therefore travels at speed c, as in
free space. In the same way we can see that a vacuum coaxial
line with perfectly conducting walls will propagate all frequencies
at speed c. In practice, the finite conductivity of the conductors
in a coaxial cable produces both attenuation and dispersion, as
does the dielectric in a normal cable, where the phase velocity
will be $v = c/\epsilon_r^{1/2}$, equation [4.25].

Recently quartz glass fibres have been developed for optical
communications over terrestrial distances by reducing their
attenuation to exceptionally low values, such as 1 dB km^{-1}.
Such an *optical fibre* acts as a dielectric waveguide with total
internal reflection at its walls achieved by applying a thin
external, dielectric coating whose refractive index is less than
that of the quartz glass (Fig. 8.7). Then from equation [5.52]
the critical value of θ is given by

$$\sin \theta_c = n_2/n_1$$

and for all $\theta > \theta_c$ the walls will be perfectly reflecting, although
an evanescent wave will penetrate the sheath. For this reason
when multiple fibres form a tight bundle they are often given a
second, opaque coating. Typically the fibre diameter is many
optical wavelengths and so the wave that propagates is a TEM
wave at phase velocity $v = c/n_1$.

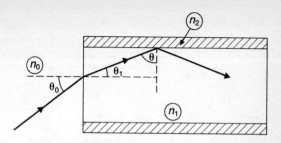

Fig. 8.7 An optical glass fibre has a core of refractive index $n_1 > n_2$, the refractive index of a thin dielectric coating, so that the light is totally internally reflected for all angles $\theta > \theta_c$, the critical angle

8.4 Cavities

Closely related to travelling waves in waveguides are standing waves in resonant cavities. The simplest cavity to analyse is a hollow, rectangular one (Fig. 8.8(a)).

Rectangular cavities

Since the cavity is bounded by conductors in all three directions, the resonant modes must satisfy the boundary conditions at three pairs of walls and equation [8.19] becomes:

$$k_x = m\frac{\pi}{a}, \ \ k_y = n\frac{\pi}{b}, \ \ k_z = l\frac{\pi}{d} \qquad [8.25]$$

for a TE_{mnl} or TM_{mnl} mode. Hence equation [8.20] is replaced by:

$$E_x = E_{0x} \cos k_x x \sin k_y y \sin k_z z \exp i\omega t$$

$$E_y = E_0 \sin \ k_x x \cos k_y y \sin k_z z \exp i\omega t$$

$$E_z = E_0 \sin k_x x \sin k_y y \cos k_z z \exp i\omega t. \qquad [8.26]$$

For a particular mode the *resonant frequency* will be, by analogy with equation [8.22],

$$v_{mnl} = \frac{c}{2} \left(\frac{m^2}{a^2} + \frac{n^2}{b^2} + \frac{l^2}{d^2} \right)^{\frac{1}{2}}.$$ [8.27]

The magnetic fields can be found from the Maxwell equation curl $\mathbf{E} = -\partial \mathbf{B}/\partial t$, or from equation [8.20] by analogy. For each resonant frequency there are two possible modes (or polarisations): a TE mode and a TM mode.

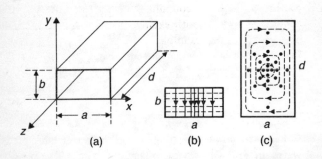

Fig.8.8 (a) Rectangular cavity, $x = a$, $y = b$, $z = d$. (b) End view. (c) Plan view, of electric $(\rightarrow, \bullet)$ and magnetic $(---)$ fields, for a TE_{101} mode

There is an infinite number of these pairs of modes, but resonant cavities are normally used in one of the lower modes, for example the TE_{101} mode (Fig. 8.8(b) and (c)). Such cavities, when used at microwave frequencies, have sharp resonances that are clearly spaced. The quality factor, or Q value, of a cavity is determined from a resonance curve similar to that shown in Fig. 4.4, where in this case the 'half-width' $2\Delta\omega$ about the resonant angular frequency ω_0 is measured at the half-power points, $(-3\mathrm{dB})$, so that:

$$Q = \omega_0/2\Delta\omega.$$ [8.28]

Typically for a 10 GHz cavity Q is 10^4–10^5.

Coupling to cavities

There is a variety of ways of exciting resonant modes in cavities

116   *Electromagnetic waves*

and, similarly, of inducing propagating waves in waveguides. Some common ones are illustrated in Fig. 8.9. A coaxial cable ending in a small antenna (wire probe) when inserted in the direction of the electric-field lines couples capacitatively to the cavity (Fig. 8.9(a)). This can be used, for example, to drive the cavity from an external oscillator. Alternatively a coaxial cable can be terminated in a small loop connected to the wall of the cavity so that the loop has its plane *normal* to the magnetic-field lines, allowing the magnetic flux to thread the loop and provide an inductive coupling (Fig. 8.9(b)). This is a particularly convenient way of both exciting a cavity and coupling out of it into a detector, for example.

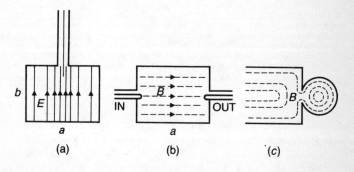

Fig. 8.9 (a) Capacitative (or electric) coupling from a coaxial cable into a cavity. (b) Inductive (or magnetic) coupling into and out of a cavity with coaxial lines. (c) Direct coupling of magnetic field in a waveguide through a small hole into a cylindrical cavity

When a waveguide has to be coupled to a cavity a simple iris in an appropriate plane can couple an electromagnetic wave from the waveguide into the resonant cavity. In Fig. 8.9(c) the plane is chosen so that the magnetic-field lines flow easily from one to the other, but in another case it could be the electric-field lines that have a common direction and provide the necessary coupling. Of course the usual requirements for impedance matching or for loose coupling have to be met.

There are many applications of resonant cavities in all branches of physics and often these are of cavities modified from the simple rectangular or cylindrical shape for particular purposes.

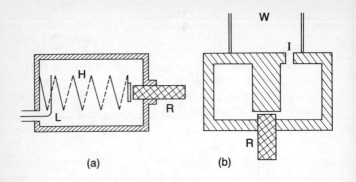

Fig. 8.10 (a) Helical resonant cavity with helix H, inductive input L and excitation of 0.1–0.5 GHz ultrasonics in the piezoelectric rod R. (b) Re-entrant cylindrical cavity with direct input through the iris I from the waveguide W and excitation of 9 GHz microsonics in the piezoelectric rod R

In the author's laboratory a common use has been to generate acoustic waves at microwave frequencies. One example is a helical cavity (Fig. 8.10(a)) where the helix greatly reduces the resonant frequency of a cavity of given size and so enables small cavities to be used for the lower microwave frequencies. Here an inductive loop L couples the incoming pulses at 0.1–0.5 GHz into the cavity, which produces a high electric field at the end of a non-resonant piezoelectric rod R and so propagates a sound wave down it. A second example is a re-entrant, cylindrical cavity (Fig. 8.10(b)), which is excited with 9 GHz pulses from a waveguide W through an iris I and similarly propagates microsonic pulses along the rod R.

Cavity radiation

There is an infinite number of resonant modes in a cavity and so it is important to calculate the total electromagnetic energy in a cavity at an absolute temperature T, assuming it to be thermally isolated and the radiation inside in thermal equilibrium with the cavity. To compute this total energy, we must find the number of modes between ν and $(\nu + d\nu)$ and for simplicity we will consider a cubical cavity, so that equation [8.27] becomes:

$$\nu_{mnl} = (m^2 + n^2 + l^2)^{1/2} c/(2a). \qquad [8.29]$$

To count the number of resonant modes, let ν_x, ν_y, ν_z form a set of coordinate axes and let each solution of equation [8.29] be a point in this frequency space. For a large volume in this space, the density of points is then $8a^3/c^3$, so that the number between spheres of radii ν and $(\nu + d\nu)$ is $4\pi\nu^2 d\nu.8a^3/c^3$. However, we have seen that for each resonant frequency there is both a TE mode and a TM mode, so that the total number of modes per unit volume between ν and $(\nu + d\nu)$ is:

$$8\pi\nu^2 d\nu/c^3. \qquad [8.30]$$

In classical statistics the principle of equipartition of energy states that each vibrational mode has an average energy of $k_B T$, where k_B is the Boltzmann constant, independent of its frequency. Therefore the energy density of cavity radiation on classical theory is:

$$u(\nu, T) = 8\pi\nu^2 k_B T/c^3 \qquad [8.31]$$

which is the *Rayleigh–Jeans law* for thermal radiation. It came as a shock to nineteenth-century physicists when they realised it led to an *infinite* total energy at a finite temperature, since

$$U(T) = \int_0^\infty u(\nu, T) \, d\nu = \frac{8\pi k_B T}{c^3} \int_0^\infty \nu^2 \, d\nu \qquad [8.32]$$

is infinite. This was known as the *ultraviolet catastrophe*, because it led to an infinite energy at the high-frequency end of the electromagnetic spectrum.

As every physics student knows, this led first Planck in 1901 and then Einstein in 1905 to the completely new concept of the quantisation of electromagnetic energy into the now familiar *photons*, but an account of the quantum theory of electromagnetic radiation must be the subject of other texts in this series.

Appendix 1
Electromagnetic quantities

Quantity	Symbol	Units	Dimensions	Equations
Electric current	I	A	A	SI unit
Electric charge	q	C	AT	[7.1]
Electric dipole moment	$\mathbf{p}$	C m	ALT	[4.7]
Electric quadrupole moment	Q	C m^2	AL^{2}T	[7.19]
Electric field	$\mathbf{E}$	V m^{-1}	A^{-1}MLT^{-3}	[2.10]
Electric potential	ϕ	V	A^{-1} ML^2 T^{-3}	[2.24]
Electrostatic energy	U	J	ML^{2}T^{-2}	[2.46]
Electric polarisation	$\mathbf{P}$	C m^{-2}	AL^{-2}T	Σ **P**/vol
Polarisability	α	F m^2	A^{2}M^{-1}T^4	[4.3]
Electric susceptibility	χ_e	—	none	[4.1]
Dielectric constant (relative permittivity)	ϵ_r	—	none	[1.25], [4.32]
Electric displacement	$\mathbf{D}$	C m^{-2}	AL^{2}T	[1.9]
Electric charge density	ρ	C m^{-3}	AL^{-3}T	q/vol
Linear charge density	λ	C m^{-1}	AL^{-1}T	q/length
Electric current density	$\mathbf{j}$	A m^{-2}	AL^{-2}	q/area/s
Surface current density	$\mathbf{i}$	A m^{-1}	AL^{-1}	[1.18]

Quantity	Symbol	Units	Dimensions	Equations
Electrical conductivity	σ	S m^{-1}	A^{-2}M^{-1}L^{-3}T^{3}	[6.1]
Magnetic field	**B**	T	A^{-1}MT^{-2}	[2.10]
Magnetic dipole moment	**m**	A m^{2}	AL^{2}	[7.14]
Magnetisation	**M**	A m^{-1}	AL^{-1}	Σ **m**/vol
Magnetising field	**H**	A m^{-1}	AL^{-1}	[1.10]
Magnetic vector potential	**A**	Wb m^{-1}	A^{-1}MLT^{-2}	[2.41]
Magnetic susceptibility	χ_m	—	none	**M/H**
Relative permeability	μ_r	—	none	[1.24]
Magnetostatic energy	U	J	$ML^{2}T^{-2}$	[2.51]
Electromagnetic energy density	u	J m^{-3}	$ML^{-1}T^{-2}$	[3.32], [5.40]
Poynting vector	$\mathscr{S}$	W m^{-2}	MT^{-3}	[3.31], [5.39]
Wave impedance	Z	Ω	A^{-2}ML^{2}T^{-3}	[3.38]
Refractive index	n	—	none	[4.26], [4.29]
Wave number	k	m^{-1}	L^{-1}	[3.10], [6.10]
Absorption coefficient	β	m^{-1}	L^{-1}	[4.31]
Skin depth	δ	m	L	[6.13]
Reflection coefficient	R	—	none	[5.45]
Transmission coefficient	T	—	none	[5.46]
Plasma frequency	ω_p	s^{-1}	T^{-1}	[6.35]
Radiation pressure	p_r	Pa (J m^{-3})	ML^{-1} T^{-2}	[6.27]
Radiated power	W	W	ML^{2} T^{-3}	[7.12]

Appendix 2
Gaussian units

The Système International d'Unités (SI) used in this book is that adopted by the General Conferences of Weights and Measures (CGPM) and endorsed by the International Organisation for Standardisation (ISO) for use by engineers and scientists throughout the world. It is based on six fundamental units: metre (m), kilogramme (kg), second (s), ampere (A), kelvin (K) and candela (cd). Such a system is, of course, arbitrary and its chief merit is that it is agreed internationally. For convenience in theoretical physics two other systems of units are often chosen: natural and Gaussian units. In the system of natural units the universal constants (h, k_B, c) are chosen to be dimensionless and of unit size, which is useful in the theory of elementary particles. In the Gaussian system the older metric units of centimetre, gram and second (c.g.s.) are retained with an electrostatic unit (e.s.u.) for electric charge and an electromagnetic unit (e.m.u.) for electric current. The ratio of current (in e.s.u.) to current (in e.m.u.) has the dimensions of a velocity and is the velocity of light *in vacuo*, c (in c.g.s. units). The net results are that ϵ_0 and μ_0 are dimensionless and of unit size in this system, leading to the replacement of $(\epsilon_0\mu_0)^{-1/2}$ by c, and that the absence of $1/4\pi$ in Coulomb's law of force leads to the presence of 4π in terms involving charges and currents. The main advantages of this system are that **E** and **B** have the same dimensions and are of equal magnitude for electromagnetic waves in free space. However, in media $\mathbf{D} = \epsilon\mathbf{E}$ and $\mathbf{B} = \mu\mathbf{H}$ and some of this simplicity is lost.

Some of the important equations in electromagnetism are given in Table A2.1 in Gaussian units, the equation number being that for SI units in the text. Conversions of some Gaussian units to SI units are given in Table A2.2, assuming $c = 3 \times 10^8$ m s^{-1}.

Table A2.1 *Electromagnetic equations in Gaussian units*

Maxwell I	div $\mathbf{E} = 4\pi\rho/\epsilon$	[1.1]; div $\mathbf{D} = 4\pi\rho$	[1.14]
Maxwell II	div $\mathbf{B} = 0$	[1.2]	
Maxwell III	curl $\mathbf{E} = -\dfrac{1}{c}\dfrac{\partial \mathbf{B}}{\partial t}$	[1.3]	
Maxwell IV	curl $\mathbf{B} = \dfrac{4\pi}{c}\mathbf{j} + \dfrac{1}{c^2}\dfrac{\partial \mathbf{E}}{\partial t}$	[1.4]; curl $\mathbf{H} = \dfrac{4\pi}{c}\mathbf{j}_f + \dfrac{1}{c}\dfrac{\partial \mathbf{D}}{\partial t}$	[1.23]
Lorentz force		$\mathbf{F} = q\left(\mathbf{E} + \dfrac{\mathbf{u} \times \mathbf{B}}{c}\right)$	[2.10]
Electric displacement		$\mathbf{D} = \mathbf{E} + 4\pi\mathbf{P}$	[1.9]
Magnetising field		$\mathbf{H} = \mathbf{B} - 4\pi\mathbf{M}$	[1.10]
Electric susceptibility		$\chi_e = \dfrac{1}{4\pi}(\epsilon - 1)$	[4.1]
Magnetic susceptibility		$\chi_m = \dfrac{1}{4\pi}(\mu - 1)$	
Energy density		$u = (1/8\pi)(\mathbf{E}.\mathbf{D} + \mathbf{B}.\mathbf{H})$	[5.40]

Table A2.2 *Conversion of Gaussian units to SI units*

Electric charge	q	3×10^9 e.s.u. = 1 coulomb
Electric current	I	1 e.m.u. = 10 ampere
Electric potential	ϕ	1 stat volt = 300 volt
Electric field	$\mathbf{E}$	3×10^4 stat volt cm^{-1} = 1 volt metre^{-1}
Electric displacement	$\mathbf{D}$	$12\pi \times 10^5$ e.s.u. cm^{-2} = 1 coulomb metre^{-2}
Energy density	u	10^{13} erg cm^{-3} = 1 joule metre^{-3}
Radiated power	W	10^7 erg second^{-1} = 1 watt
Resistance	R	1 stat ohm = 9×10^{11} ohm
Capacitance	C	9×10^{11} cm = 1 farad
Inductance	L	10^9 e.m.u. = 1 henry
Magnetic field	$\mathbf{B}$	10^4 gauss = 1 tesla
Magnetising field	$\mathbf{H}$	$4\pi \times 10^{-3}$ oersted = 1 ampere metre^{-1}

Appendix 3
Physical constants

Constant	Symbol	Value
Electric constant	$\epsilon_0 = 1/(\mu_0 c^2)$	8.85×10^{-12} F m^{-1}
Magnetic constant	μ_0	$4\pi \times 10^{-7}$ H m^{-1}
Speed of light	c	3.00×10^8 m s^{-1}
Electronic charge	e	1.60×10^{-19} C
Rest mass of electron	m_e	9.11×10^{-31} kg
Rest mass of proton	m_p	1.67×10^{-27} kg
Planck constant	h	6.63×10^{-34} J s
	$\hbar = h/2\pi$	1.05×10^{-34} J s
Boltzmann constant	k_B	1.38×10^{-23} J K^{-1}
Avogadro number	N_A	6.02×10^{23} mol^{-1}
Gravitation constant	G	6.67×10^{-11} N m^2 kg^{-}
Bohr radius	$a_0 = \dfrac{4\pi\epsilon_0 \hbar^2}{m_e^{\,2}}$	5.29×10^{-11} m
Bohr magneton	$\mu_B = \dfrac{e\hbar}{2m_e}$	9.27×10^{-24} J T^{-1}
Electron volt	eV	1.60×10^{-19} J
Molar volume at S.T.P.	V_m	2.24×10^{-2} m^3 mol^{-1}
Acceleration due to gravity	g	9.81 m s^{-2}

Appendix 4
Vector calculus

For general vectors $\mathbf{A}$, $\mathbf{B}$ and a scalar Ω.

Identities

$$\text{div}\,(\Omega\mathbf{A}) = \Omega\,\text{div}\,\mathbf{A} + \mathbf{A}.\text{grad}\,\Omega \qquad [A4.1]$$

$$\text{div}\,(\mathbf{A}\times\mathbf{B}) = \mathbf{B}.\text{curl}\,\mathbf{A} - \mathbf{A}.\text{curl}\,\mathbf{B} \qquad [A4.2]$$

$$\text{curl}\,(\Omega\mathbf{A}) = \Omega\,\text{curl}\,\mathbf{A} + \text{grad}\,\Omega\times\mathbf{A} \qquad [A4.3]$$

$$\text{curl}\,\text{grad}\,\Omega = 0 \qquad [A4.4]$$

$$\text{div}\,\text{curl}\,\mathbf{A} = 0 \qquad [A4.5]$$

$$\text{curl}\,\text{curl}\,\mathbf{A} = \text{grad}\,\text{div}\,\mathbf{A} - \nabla^2\mathbf{A} \qquad [A4.6]$$

Cartesian differential operators

$$\text{grad}\,\Omega = \nabla\Omega = \frac{\partial\Omega}{\partial x}\hat{\mathbf{i}} + \frac{\partial\Omega}{\partial y}\hat{\mathbf{j}} + \frac{\partial\Omega}{\partial z}\hat{\mathbf{k}} \qquad [A4.7]$$

$$\text{div}\,\mathbf{A} = \nabla.\mathbf{A} = \frac{\partial A_x}{\partial x} + \frac{\partial A_y}{\partial y} + \frac{\partial A_z}{\partial z} \qquad [A4.8]$$

$$\text{curl}\,\mathbf{A} = \nabla\times\mathbf{A} = \begin{vmatrix} \hat{\mathbf{i}} & \hat{\mathbf{j}} & \hat{\mathbf{k}} \\ \partial/\partial x & \partial/\partial y & \partial/\partial z \\ A_x & A_y & A_z \end{vmatrix} \qquad [A4.9]$$

$$\text{div}\,(\text{grad}) = \nabla^2 = \frac{\partial^2}{\partial x^2} + \frac{\partial^2}{\partial y^2} + \frac{\partial^2}{\partial z^2} \qquad [A4.10]$$

Spherical polar differential operators

$$\text{grad } \Omega = \frac{\partial \Omega}{\partial r}\,\hat{\mathbf{r}} + \frac{1}{r}\frac{\partial \Omega}{\partial \theta}\,\hat{\boldsymbol{\theta}} + \frac{1}{r \sin \theta}\frac{\partial \Omega}{\partial \psi}\,\hat{\boldsymbol{\psi}} \qquad [A4.11]$$

$$\text{div } \mathbf{A} = \frac{1}{r^2}\frac{\partial}{\partial r}(r^2 A_r) + \frac{1}{r \sin \theta}\frac{\partial}{\partial \theta}(A_0 \sin \theta)$$

$$+ \frac{1}{r \sin \theta}\frac{\partial A_\psi}{\partial \psi} \qquad [A4.12]$$

$$\text{curl } \mathbf{A} = \frac{1}{r^2 \sin \theta}\begin{vmatrix} \hat{\mathbf{r}} & r\hat{\boldsymbol{\theta}} & r \sin \theta\,\hat{\boldsymbol{\psi}} \\[2mm] \partial/\partial r & \partial/\partial \theta & \partial/\partial \psi \\[2mm] A_r & rA_\theta & r \sin \theta A_\psi \end{vmatrix} \qquad [A4.13]$$

$$\nabla^2 = \frac{1}{r^2}\frac{\partial}{\partial r}\left(r^2\frac{\partial}{\partial r}\right) + \frac{1}{r^2 \sin \theta}\frac{\partial}{\partial \theta}\left(\sin \theta\frac{\partial}{\partial \theta}\right) + \frac{1}{r^2 \sin^2 \theta}\frac{\partial^2}{\partial \psi^2}$$
$$[A4.14]$$

Cylindrical polar differential operators

$$\text{grad } \Omega = \frac{\partial \Omega}{\partial r}\,\hat{\mathbf{r}} + \frac{\partial \Omega}{r\partial \theta}\,\hat{\boldsymbol{\theta}} + \frac{\partial \Omega}{\partial z}\,\hat{\mathbf{z}} \qquad [A4.15]$$

$$\text{div } \mathbf{A} = \frac{1}{r}\frac{\partial}{\partial r}(rA_r) + \frac{\partial A_\theta}{r\partial \theta} + \frac{\partial A_z}{\partial z} \qquad [A4.16]$$

$$\text{curl } \mathbf{A} = \frac{1}{r}\begin{vmatrix} \hat{\mathbf{r}} & r\hat{\boldsymbol{\theta}} & \hat{\mathbf{z}} \\[2mm] \partial/\partial r & \partial/\partial \theta & \partial/\partial z \\[2mm] A_r & rA_\theta & A_z \end{vmatrix} \qquad [A4.17]$$

$$\nabla^2 = \frac{1}{r}\frac{\partial}{\partial r}\left(r\frac{\partial}{\partial r}\right) + \frac{1}{r^2}\frac{\partial^2}{\partial \theta^2} + \frac{\partial^2}{\partial z^2}\,. \qquad [A4.18]$$

Theorems

For a smoothly varying vector field **A**.

Gauss's divergence theorem

$$\int_S \mathbf{A}.\mathbf{dS} = \int_V \text{div } \mathbf{A} \, d\tau \qquad [A4.19]$$

where the surface S encloses the volume V, $\mathbf{dS} = \hat{\mathbf{n}}dS$ is a vector of magnitude dS along the outward normal $\hat{\mathbf{n}}$ to the surface dS and $d\tau$ is an element of the volume V.

Stokes's theorem

$$\oint_C \mathbf{A}.\mathbf{ds} = \int_S (\text{curl } \mathbf{A}).\mathbf{dS} \qquad [A4.20]$$

where the closed loop C bounds the surface S and $\mathbf{ds}$ is a vector element of the loop C.

Appendix 5
Lorentz transformations

The transformation of physical quantities from an inertial frame S (the laboratory frame) to a frame S' moving with respect to S at a speed u in the positive x direction is given in Cartesian coordinates, where $\beta = u/c$ and $\gamma = (1 - \beta^2)^{-\frac{1}{2}}$. For the inverse transforms replace u by $-u$. (See also Chapter 2 and Fig. 2.1.)

Coordinates

$$x' = \gamma (x - ut), y' = y, z' = z, t' = \gamma \left\{ t - \left(\frac{\beta}{c} \right) x \right\} \quad [A5.1]$$

Velocities

$$v_x' = \frac{v_x - u}{\{1 - (\beta/c)v_x\}}, v_y' = \frac{v_y}{\gamma\{1 - (\beta/c)v_x\}}, v_z' = \frac{v_z}{\gamma\{1 - (\beta/c)v_x\}}$$

$$[A5.2]$$

Components of a force

$$F_x' = F_x - \frac{(\beta/c)(v_y F_y + v_z F_z)}{\{1 - (\beta/c)v_x\}} \quad [A5.3]$$

$$F_y' = \frac{F_y}{\gamma\{1 - (\beta/c)v_x\}} \quad [A5.4]$$

$$F_z' = \frac{F_z}{\gamma\{1 - (\beta/c)v_x\}}. \quad [A5.5]$$

Electric field

$$E_x' = E_x , \ E_y' = \gamma(E_y - \beta cB_z), \ E_z' = \gamma(E_z + \beta cB_y)$$

[A5.6]

Magnetic field

$$B_x' = B_x, B_y' = \gamma\{B_y + (\beta/c)E_z\} , B_z' = \gamma\{B_z - (\beta/c)E_y\}$$

[A5.7]

For further information, see *Relativity Physics* by R.E. Turner in this series.

Appendix 6
Exercises

Chapter 2

1   Use the Lorentz transformations for the components of a force, of a velocity and of the coordinates, given in Appendix 5, to show that the Coulomb force $\mathbf{F}'$ on a moving charge in a moving frame, equation [2.14], transforms into the Lorentz force $\mathbf{F}$, equation [2.15], in the laboratory frame.

2   A narrow beam of electrons of energy 7 GeV is circulating in a large storage ring. What are the maximum instantaneous values of the electric and magnetic fields due to each electron at a distance of 5 mm from the beam and in which direction is each vector relative to the beam?

3   Show that the vector potential at a point P, distance $\mathbf{r}$ from the centre of a thin, circular wire carrying a persistent current I, is:

$$\mathbf{A}(\mathbf{r}) = \frac{\mu_0 I}{4\pi} \oint \frac{\mathbf{dl}}{R}$$

where R is the distance from the circuit element $\mathbf{dl}$ to P and $r \gg a$, the radius of the circle. Hence show that:

$$\mathbf{A}(\mathbf{r}) = \frac{\mu_0 \, (\mathbf{m} \times \mathbf{r})}{4\pi r^3}$$

where $\mathbf{m}$ is the magnetic dipole moment of the circular current I.

4   Using the definitions of $\mathbf{A}$ and ϕ given in equations [2.26] and [2.29], show that Maxwell's equations div $\mathbf{D} = \rho_f$ and curl $\mathbf{H} = \mathbf{j}_f + \partial \mathbf{D}/\partial t$ lead to the following inhomogeneous wave equations for a linear, isotropic medium of permittivity ϵ and permeability μ:

$$\nabla^2 \mathbf{A} = -\epsilon\mu \frac{\partial^2 \mathbf{A}}{\partial t^2} = -\mu \mathbf{j}_f$$

$$\nabla^2 \phi = -\epsilon\mu \frac{\partial^2 \phi}{\partial t^2} = -\frac{\rho_f}{\epsilon}.$$

5   Explain why the electric field due to a charge is not given by the force per unit charge, nor the gradient of its electric potential, when the charge is moving.

Chapter 3

1   Show that the displacement current density in a linearly polarised plane wave $\mathbf{E} = \mathbf{E_0} \exp i(\omega - \mathbf{k.r})$ is $i\epsilon_0 \omega \mathbf{E}$ and calculate its root mean square value when $E_0 = 5.1$ mV m^{-1} and $\omega/2\pi = 1$ GHz.

2   A stationary observer is looking at a mirror that is travelling away from him at a speed $v < c$. Show that if he shines a laser beam of frequency ν at the moving mirror he will see a reflected frequency:

$$\nu' = \nu \{ (1 - v/c)/(1 + v/c) \}^{\frac{1}{2}}.$$

3   Solar energy falls on the earth's surface at about 1 kW m^{-2}. Estimate the r.m.s. electric and magnetic fields in the sunshine received.

4   Assuming that the earth's magnetic field is due to a dipole at its centre which produces a field of 15 mT at the North Pole, estimate the total magnetic energy in the earth's external magnetic field.

5   A radio antenna at the surface of the earth is emitting its radiation radially. If its average power is 20 kW, what is the energy flux at a domestic receiver 50 km away? What are the r.m.s. values of the $\mathbf{E}$ and $\mathbf{H}$ fields at the receiver?

Chapter 4

1   A charge q, mass m, oscillating with amplitude a at an angular frequency ω_0 radiates energy at a rate $(\mu_0 q^2 \omega_0^4 a^2)/(12\pi c)$. By solving the equation of motion of a harmonically bound charge, subject to a damping force proportional to its speed and driven by a force $F \exp(i\omega t)$, find the mean energy of the oscillator and hence show that the damping constant which

simulates the radiation is $\gamma = (2\pi\mu_0 cq^2)/(3m\lambda_0^2)$, where $\lambda_0 = 2\pi\, c/\omega_0$. Estimate the natural width due to this cause of a line in an atomic emission spectrum.

2 Show, from Maxwell's equations, that the wave equations for a polarisable, magnetisable dielectric of relative permittivity ϵ_r and relative permeability μ_r are:

$$\nabla^2 \mathbf{E} = \frac{1}{v^2}\frac{\partial^2 \mathbf{E}}{\partial t^2}, \quad \nabla^2 \mathbf{B} = \frac{1}{v^2}\frac{\partial^2 \mathbf{B}}{\partial t^2}$$

where $v = c\,(\mu_r\epsilon_r)^{-\frac{1}{2}}$.

3 The electric vector of an electromagnetic wave in a dielectric is:

$$E_x = E_0 \exp\,(-\beta z)\exp i\omega\,(t - n_R z/c)$$

where β is the absorption coefficient. Show that the magnetic vector is perpendicular to E_x and find the phase difference between the vectors.

Chapter 5

1 Estimate the reflectance and transmittance at normal incidence for (a) light and (b) radio waves from air into water. How can you explain this microscopically?

2 Show that the reflection coefficient for radiation at normal incidence from free space on to a plane surface of material of refractive index $(n_R - in_I)$ is:

$$R = \frac{(n_R - 1)^2 + n_I^2}{(n_R + 1)^2 + n_I^2}.$$

For a metal at low frequencies $(\omega/2\pi)$ and conductivity σ

$$(n_R - in_I)^2 = -i\sigma/(\omega\epsilon_0).$$

Show that $R = 1 - (8\omega\epsilon_0/\sigma)^{\frac{1}{2}}$ when $\sigma \gg \omega\epsilon_0$.

3 A transparent dielectric of refractive index n has a plane boundary, forming the (y, z) plane, with free space. A linearly polarised plane wave is incident on the boundary from the medium. The magnetic field $\mathbf{B}$ in the incident (I), reflected (R) and transmitted (T) beams is parallel to the positive axis and has components:

$$B_I = A \exp \left[i\omega \{ t - n(x \cos \alpha + y \sin \alpha)/c \} \right]$$

$$B_R = B \exp \left[i\omega \{ t - n(-x \cos \alpha' + y \sin \alpha')/c \} \right]$$

$$B_T = C \exp \left[i\omega \{ t - (x \cos \beta + y \sin \beta)/c \} \right]$$

Draw a diagram showing the directions of the three beams and of their electric fields, indicating the angles α, α' and β. By considering the y-dependence of $\mathbf{B}$ at the surface, show that $\alpha = \alpha'$ and $\sin \beta = n \sin \alpha$. Show that a solution of the equation $\sin \beta = n \sin \alpha$ can be obtained when $n \sin \alpha > 1$ by putting $\beta = \pi/2 + i\delta$, where $\cosh \delta = n \sin \alpha$. If $n = 1.4$, $\alpha = 80°$ and the radiation has wavelength of 400 nm in free space, find how far from the surface the magnetic field has dropped to 10% of its value at the surface. [Hint: $\sin(\gamma + i\delta) = \sin \gamma \cosh \delta + i \cos \gamma \sinh \delta$; $\cos(\gamma + i\delta) = \cos \gamma \cosh \delta - i \sin \gamma \sinh \delta$.]

4 A laser beam, having a power of 100 MW and a diameter of 1 mm, passes through a glass window of refractive index 1.59. Find the peak values of the electric and magnetic fields of the laser beam (a) in the air, (b) in the glass.

5 Show that the wave impedance Z of a medium of permeability μ and permittivity ϵ is $(\mu/\epsilon)^{1/2}$.

6 A uniform plane wave is normally incident from a medium 1 into a parallel slab of thickness l of medium 2 and emerges into medium 3 after two partial reflections. Show that there are no reflections: (a) when media 1 and 3 are the same and $k_2 l = m\pi$, where m is an integer; (b) when $k_2 l = \pi/2$ and $Z_2 = (Z_1 Z_3)^{1/2}$.

Chapter 6

1 Show that an electromagnetic wave with complex $\mathbf{E}$ and $\mathbf{H}$ fields given by $\mathbf{E} = (\mathbf{E_R} + i\mathbf{E_I}) \exp i\omega t$ and $\mathbf{H} = (\mathbf{H_R} + i\mathbf{H_I}) \exp i\omega t$, has an average Poynting vector given by $\langle \mathscr{S} \rangle = \frac{1}{2} \operatorname{Re}(\mathbf{E} \times \mathbf{H^*})$, where $\mathbf{H^*}$ is the complex conjugate of $\mathbf{H}$.

2 A linearly polarised electromagnetic wave falls at normal incidence on a good conductor. Show from the Lorentz force $\mathbf{j} \times \mathbf{B}$ due to its magnetic vector $\mathbf{B}$ acting on the induced surface current $\mathbf{j}_f$ in a direction normal to the surface that it produces a radiation

pressure $p_r = 2u_i$, where u_i is the energy density of the incident wave.

3   Electromagnetic waves of frequency 1 MHz are incident normally on a sheet of pure copper at $0°C$. (a) Calculate the depth in the copper at which the amplitude of the wave has been reduced to half its value at the surface, if the conductivity of copper at $0°C$ $= 6.4 \times 10^7$ S m^{-1}. (b) Explain how you could calculate this depth at higher frequencies and at lower temperatures.

4   Discuss the possibility of using radio waves to communicate with a submarine submerged in seawater of conductivity 4.0 S m^{-1}.

5   A spacecraft returning to earth produces a cloud of ionised atoms of density 10^{15} m^{-3}. Find (a) the plasma frequency of this cloud, (b) the cut-off wavelength for communication with the ground.

6   Show that the energy dissipated by a current I flowing in a long, straight wire of conductivity σ and radius a can be described as flowing into it radially from its surroundings. Hence show that the power dissipated per unit length is $I^2/(\pi\sigma a^2)$.

Chapter 7

1   Using the Lorentz condition for the vector potential **A** show that the equation:

$$\frac{\partial A_z}{\partial z} = \left(\frac{\mu_0 l}{4\pi}\right) \frac{\partial}{\partial z}\left\{\frac{I_0}{r} \cos \omega (t-r/c)\right\}$$

can be solved to find the scalar potential:

$$\phi = \frac{l}{4\pi\epsilon_0}\left\{\frac{\cos\theta}{r^2} q_0 \sin\omega(t-r/c) + \frac{\cos\theta}{cr} I_0 \cos\omega(t-c/r)\right\}$$

where l, r, z, θ are given in Fig. 7.1(b) and $I_0 = \omega q_0$. .

2   For the radiation field of a Hertzian dipole the vector potential is:

$$\mathbf{A}(r, t) = \frac{\mu_0 l I_0}{4\pi r}\left\{\cos\omega(t-r/c)\right\}(\cos\theta\hat{r} - \sin\theta\hat{\theta})$$

and the scalar potential is given in exercise 1. Show that the electric vector is $\mathbf{E} = E_\theta \hat{\theta}$, where $E_\theta = -E_0 r^{-1} \sin\omega(t-r/c)$ and $E_0 = (\omega l I_0 \sin\theta)/(4\pi\epsilon_0 c^2)$.

3   The Poynting vector for the radiation field of a Hertzian dipole is:

$$\mathscr{S} = \frac{E_0{}^2}{\mu_0 c r^2} \sin^2 \omega \, (t - r/c) \hat{\mathbf{r}}$$

Show that the average Poynting vector over one cycle is:

$$\langle \mathscr{S} \rangle = \frac{\mu_0 c l^2}{32\pi^2} I_0{}^2 \sin^2 \theta \, \frac{k^2}{r^2} \hat{\mathbf{r}}$$

where I_0 is given in exercise 1 and $k = \omega/c$.

4   Show that the radiation resistance of a current-loop antenna of radius a is $20\pi^2 (ka)^4$, where k is the wave number of the radiation. Estimate the radiation resistance for a loop with the Bohr radius a_0 emitting red light.

5   Show that the power radiated by a linear quadrupole antenna (Fig. 7.3(a)) is given by $(\mu_0 \omega^6 Q_0{}^2)/(240\pi c^3)$ and that its radiation resistance is $4 (kl)^4$. Hence show that the ratio of the power radiated from a quadrupole antenna to that from a Hertzian dipole of the same length is $(kl)^2/20$.

6   The radiation field of a Hertzian dipole of moment $\mathbf{p}\,(t) = \mathbf{p}_0 \exp i\omega t$ has vector potential:

$$\mathbf{A}\,(\mathbf{r}, t) = \frac{\mu_0}{4\pi r} [\dot{p}] \, (\cos \theta \hat{\mathbf{r}} - \sin \theta \hat{\boldsymbol{\theta}})$$

where $[\dot{p}]$ is the time derivative at the reduced time $(t - r/c)$ of p. Show that the radiation fields are:

$$E_\theta = \frac{\sin \theta}{4\pi\epsilon_0 c^2 r} [\ddot{p}], \quad B_\psi = \frac{\mu_0 \sin \theta}{4\pi c r} [\ddot{p}]$$

and that the power radiated is $W = [\ddot{p}]^2/(6\pi\epsilon_0 c^3)$.

Chapter 8

1   For the TE_{10} mode in a lossless, rectangular waveguide (Fig. 8.3(a)), obtain expressions for (a) the average electrical energy, (b) the average magnetic energy, per unit length of guide, and hence show that the total electromagnetic energy per unit length is $E_0{}^2 \epsilon_0 ab/4$, where E_0 is the peak amplitude of the electric vector.

2   Calculate the cut-off frequency of the following modes in a rectangular waveguide of internal dimensions 30 mm $\times$ 10 mm:

TE_{01}, TE_{10}, TM_{11}, TM_{21}. Hence show that this waveguide will only propagate the TE_{10} mode of 10 GHz radiation.

3   A rectangular cavity has internal dimensions (in mm) of 30 × 15 × 45. Find the three lowest resonant modes and calculate their frequencies.

4   A microwave receiver is connected by 30 m of waveguide of internal cross-section 23 mm × 10 mm to an antenna. Find the ratio of (a) the phase velocity and (b) the signal velocity in the waveguide to that in free space, for reception at 12 GHz.

5   A rectangular cavity made from waveguide of aspect ratio 2.25:1 resonates at 8.252, 9.067 and 9.967 GHz. If these frequencies are those of adjacent TE_{10l} modes find the length of the cavity, assuming that the cut-off frequency of the TE_{10} mode of the waveguide is 6.56 GHz.

Appendix 7
Answers to exercises

Chapter 2

2   $E = 0.78$ V m^{-1}, radial; $B = 2.6 \times 10^{-9}$ T, azimuthal.

Chapter 3

1   200 μA m^{-2}.
3   600 V m^{-1}; 2 μT.
4   10^{19} J.
5   1.27 μW m^{-2}; 22 mV m^{-1}; 58 μA m^{-1}

Chapter 4

1   1.2×10^{-14} m.
3   $\tan \delta = n_I/n_R$.

Chapter 5

1   (a) R = 2%; T = 98%; (b) R = 64%, T = 36%; interference between radiation induced and incident.
3   153 nm.
4   (a) 312 MV m^{-1}, 1.04 T; (b) 248 MV m^{-1}, 1.31 T.

Chapter 6

3   (a) 44 μm.
4   At 100 Hz, skin depth = 25 m.
5   (a) 280 MHz; (b) 1.1 m.

Chapter 7

4 10^{-11} Ω.

Chapter 8

1 (a) $E_0{}^2 \epsilon_0 ab/8$; (b) same.
2 15, 5, 15.8, 18.0 GHz.
3 101, 102, 201; 6.0, 8.3, 10.5 GHz.
4 (a) 1.19, (b) 0.84.
5 119.8 mm.

INDEX

Index

RELATIVITY PHYSICS

Relativity Physics covers all the material required for a first course in relativity. Beginning with an examination of the paradoxes that arose in applying the principle of relativity to the two great pillars of nineteenth-century physics—classical mechanics and electromagnetism—Dr Turner shows how Einstein resolved these problems in a spectacular and brilliantly intuitive way. The implications of Einstein's postulates are then discussed and the book concludes with a discussion of the charged particle in the electromagnetic field.

The text incorporates details of the most recent experiments and includes applications to high-energy physics, astronomy, and solid state physics. Exercises with answers are included for the student.

R. E. Turner

Dr Roy Turner is Reader in Theoretical Physics at the University of Sussex.

ISBN 0-7102-0001-3
About 128 pp., 198 mm x 129 mm, diagrams, April 1984

CLASSICAL MECHANICS

A course in classical mechanics is an essential requirement of any first degree course in physics. In this volume Dr Brian Cowan provides a clear, concise and self-contained introduction to the subject and covers all the material needed by a student taking such a course. The author treats the material from a modern viewpoint, culminating in a final chapter showing how the Lagrangian and Hamiltonian formulations lend themselves particularly well to the more 'modern' areas of physics such as quantum mechanics. Worked examples are included in the text and there are exercises, with answers, for the student.

B. P. Cowan

Dr Brian Cowan is in the Department of Physics, Bedford College, University of London

ISBN 0-7102-0280-6
About 128 pp., diagrams, 129 mm x 198 mm, April 1984

ELECTRICITY AND MAGNETISM

Electromagnetism is basic to our understanding of the properties of matter and yet is often regarded a difficult part of a first degree course. In this book Professor Dobbs provides a concise and elegant account of the subject, covering all the material required by a student taking such a course. Although concentrating on the essentials of the subject, interesting applications are discussed in the text. Vector operators are introduced at the appropriate points and exercises, with answers, are included for the student.

E. R. Dobbs

Professor Roland Dobbs is Hildred Carlile Professor of Physics at the University of London.

ISBN 0-7102-0157-5
About 128 pp., 198 mm x 129 mm, diagrams, April 1984